BREW IT
YOURSELF

BREW IT
YOURSELF

NICK MOYLE & RICHARD HOOD

CAMERON + COMPANY
Petaluma, California

For Roscoe and Tilly

CAMERON + COMPANY
6 Petaluma Blvd. North, Suite B-6,
Petaluma, CA 94952
707-769-1617
www.cameronbooks.com

Publisher: Chris Gruener
Creative Director: Iain R. Morris
Additional Design: Suzi Hutsell

This edition published in 2016
by Cameron + Company, Inc.

First published in the USA and Canada
in 2015 by Nourish, an imprint of
Watkins Media Limited
19 Cecil Court
London WC2N 4HE

Publisher: Grace Cheetham
Project Manager: Rebecca Woods
Editor: Liz Jones
Americanizer: Whitefox Publishing
Head of Design: Georgina Hewitt
Designers & Food Stylists: Nick Moyle and Richard Hood
Production: Uzma Taj
Cover Illustration: Jade Wheaton

Typeset in Aller and LunchBox

ISBN: 978-1-937359-97-3

10 9 8 7 6 5 4 3 2 1

Printed in China

Publish Notes on the Recipes

Unless otherwise stated:
• Use large eggs
• Use medium fruit and vegetables
• Use fresh ingredients, including herbs and spices
• 1 tsp. = 5ml   1 tbsp. = 15ml   1 cup = 240ml

Publisher's Note

While every care has been taken in compiling the recipes
for this book, Watkins Media Limited, Cameron + Company,
or any other persons who have been involved in working
on this publication, cannot accept responsibility for any
errors or omissions, inadvertent or not, that may be found
in the recipes or text, nor for any problems that may arise
as a result of preparing one of these recipes. If you are
pregnant or breastfeeding or have any special dietary
requirements or medical conditions, it is advisable to
consult a medical professional before following any of the
recipes contained in this book.

CONTENTS

FOREWORD

For too long, the making of "homebrew" has been a pastime more commonly associated with folk of a certain age: those that favor sandal/sock combinations and hairy sweaters. Seen as a 70s throwback, this genteel pastime has long been mocked by the ignorant and uninformed.

This is all about to change . . .

We have bravely taken it upon ourselves to brew, ferment and infuse vast amounts of drinks from ingredients foraged, grown and scavenged in our gardens, on our allotment and sometimes—whisper it—from the store.

Along the way, we have created gastronomic disasters too awful to recount, but that has all been part of the learning process. And we did it for you.

This book contains a selection of our very best recipes, designed for a new generation of home brewers. It will provide inspiration for you to turn your own surplus harvest into tasty alcoholic beverages, explain how foraged ingredients can transform ordinary drinks into something wonderful, and demonstrate how anyone can create their own uniquely flavored booze. This book will debunk myths, celebrate experimentation and take the fear out of the science of fermentation.

With ingredients varying from parsnips to pears and dandelions to damsons, we'll be furiously fermenting, boldly brewing and magically mixing a weird and wonderful array of alcoholic drinks.

Rise up, embrace the carboy and join us on our homebrew odyssey . . . it's going to be one garden party you won't want to miss!

The Two Thirsty Gardeners

THE BREW-IT-YOURSELF
MANIFESTO

You don't have to be a science expert or a Michelin-starred chef to get fantastic results through making your own booze, but we do try to follow a few guidelines to maximize the merriment.

Here is our simple manifesto, which we have nailed to the door of our brewing shed to keep us on the straight and narrow.

● Experiment! Swap ingredients to invent recipes, change base spirits in your liqueurs and add herbs and spices to just about anything. Try fermenting unusual produce . . . that unwanted vegetable lurking in the corner? It might just work!

● Make copious notes, and keep them safe. All of your experimenting will go to waste if they are accidentally mixed up with the recycling, riding on the back of a cereal packet.

● Taste is subjective. Remember, one person's Chablis is another person's drain cleaner.

● Don't get hung up over quantities. Treat measurements as a rough guide. Slightly more or less is rarely a problem.

● Homegrown or foraged ingredients are best, but stores offer alternatives. There is no shame in purchasing produce in the pursuit of boozy beverages.

● Sometimes being patient will reward you with improved drinks, but if it tastes good, enjoy it early.

● Be generous and share your drinks. Receive feedback and take criticism graciously, no matter how misguided it may be.

● ALWAYS treat alcohol with respect. Your hard work deserves it.

BREW-IT-YOURSELF: THE BASICS

To make decent booze you need decent ingredients. The freshest, most flavorsome produce will always reward you with a higher quality of drink. We go into more detail about some of our favorite ingredients later, but here we'll deal with the three main ways of acquiring them: grow them yourself, track them down when foraging . . . or buy them.

GROWING YOUR OWN

A lot of people begin their brewing journeys when they realize that surplus homegrown produce can be converted into alcohol. We know many gardeners with substantial rhubarb plants who are harvesting stalks long after they've tired of rhubarab pies, but don't know what else to do with them. Point out how easy rhubarb wine is to make and there's a good chance they'll soon be scouring garage sales for their first carboy.

Turning homegrown produce into tasty beverages is a hugely rewarding experience. And unlike most forms of cooking, where your hard-grown food is cooked and gobbled within hours, a bottle of booze will keep those flavors preserved for weeks, months and even years.

WHAT TO GROW

What you're able to grow will depend largely on where you live and how much space you have. But even people without a yard can often manage a few pots of herbs on a windowsill, which can go into any number of drinks.

If you've got more space outdoors, you have a few more choices. Among the considerations for plant selection might be the following:

• What will save me money?
• What can I grow that's hard to buy?
• What's the most versatile?
• How much cost and effort will it take to grow?
• What will give me the biggest harvest?

These answers will be different from person to person, but we're certain that whatever criteria you base your decision on you'll enjoy the resulting booze just that little bit more.

FORAGING

Growing your own ingredients is rewarding, but foraging for them can be even better. Nature has done all the hard graft of sowing and nurturing, leaving you to grab the spoils for free.

Foraging puts you back at one with nature and takes you down seasonal brewing paths that have been followed by generations of home brewers. For us, few sights are more exciting than the mass arrival of elderflowers, signaling the start of summer and a long season of increased fermenting and infusing activities. When fall arrives, a whole new selection of fruit and berry flavors will send brewing addicts into a giddy spin—we struggle to complete any car journey without emitting excitable yelps every time we drive past a previously undetected apple tree.

WHAT TO FORAGE

It's obvious, but worth reinforcing, that many wild plants are poisonous, so only pick what you're 100 percent certain is edible. Fortunately some of the most abundant foragable goods are easy to identify, making them worthy of a boozy dabble—leaves from mighty oak and beech trees, spruce needles and the common weeds dandelion and nettle all fall into this category.

Many wild flowers are edible and make interesting flavors for wines and infusions. If you want to test to see if you like a particular flower in a boozy context, start with quick sparkling drinks before progressing to wine.

Some roots, such as dandelion and burdock, are worth looking out for—although you should seek permission from landowners if you're considering taking the garden fork with you. Berries can often be harder to identify, as many species have poisonous lookalikes, so take extra care. However blackberries, elderberries, sloes and damsons should be familiar to most people.

GOOD FORAGING PRACTICE

It's important to look after nature and, in return, she'll continue to provide you with bountiful brewing goods. Try not to damage plants when picking, and don't strip bare the first tree or bush you see—many birds and mammals rely on these same fruits for survival, so make sure to leave enough to go around.

WHERE TO LOOK

If you want to use a specific ingredient, it's worth finding out what kind of environment best suits that particular plant before heading out into the wild. If you prefer to wander in a more aimless manner and leave your harvest to chance, then the edges of thoroughfares—particularly railways, rivers and abandoned paths—can be the most rewarding. The thin natural boundaries between routeway and cultivated land have often been left untouched for decades, meaning that any foragable goods will be well established. They're also zones in which discarded fruit seeds lie undisturbed to germinate and grow, creating mini orchards ready to be plundered.

SHOPPING

There are numerous ingredients you'll have to buy, including essentials such as sugar, yeast and spirits for infusing, plus most of the basic grains used in our beer recipes. And despite our advocacy of homegrown or foraged foods, there's no reason why you shouldn't use store-bought ingredients for everything you make.

Not even the very best horticulturalist is likely to have access to an all-year-round harvest for all drink types, and shops can fill in the seasonal growing gaps. For us that means imported citrus fruits, dried fruit and even canned food in the winter months.

It's also worth tracking down your nearest homebrew store or a suitable online equivalent. Besides selling essential equipment, a range of sterilizing chemicals, yeast and other specialist brewing ingredients, you might be lucky enough to find that they stock other treats such as dried fruit and flowers (including elder and rose) and an interesting array of fresh hops.

Beyond these specialist stores and grocery stores you should also acquaint yourself with local farm stores, apothecaries, herbalists and health food stores for as wide a range of buying choices as possible.

GET STARTED MAKING BOOZE

So you've sourced your ingredients, have a raging thirst and are all set to brew. Before you plow headlong into our recipes, there are a few considerations to ensure that all your hard work doesn't end up being poured down the drain in a giant sulk. We've gone into detail on the requirements for each drinks style at the start of each section; before you get that far it's worth doing a bit of general cramming.

STERILIZATION

We'll start with THE most tedious part of the process, but arguably the most important. Months of work can be wasted by contamination from a dirty bottle or piece of equipment, so all items that come in contact with your precious brew—before, during and after making it—must be cleaned thoroughly before use.

There are various chemicals on the market that will do this (our choice is VWP Cleaner, available in powdered form from homebrew stores in various sizes of tub). To sterilize your kit simply dissolve the powder in warm water following the pack instructions, and briefly soak everything that will come into contact with your drinks in the solution before rinsing it through with water. The rinsing stage is important, as chemical aftertastes can taint a brew just as effectively as a grubby funnel. It is also wise, though not vital, to sterilize your hard cider- and wine-making ingredients to kill off unwanted yeasts and bacteria before any fermentation begins. This can be achieved by dropping a Campden tablet (which needs crushing; two teaspoons make perfect crushers) into your ingredients 24 hours before adding the yeast. This can also help ward off oxidization, so Campden tablets are often added to wine before bottling. However, Campden tablets come with a cautionary note: they're made up of sodium metabisulfite, which one out of every 100 people is sensitive to (the effects cause asthma-like symptoms)—hence the "contains sulfites" warning on many wine and hard cider labels. You should check with your guests before sharing any sulfited drinks.

For drinks that don't involve fermentation, cleanliness is still important, and it's always worth sterilizing glass storage bottles before topping them up with your booze. Wash and rinse in hot water before drying them out in an oven set to around 250°F. And remember—don't add cold liquids to hot glass (or vice versa), because the glass might crack.

SUGAR

Most of our recipes include the addition of sugar to raise the alcohol level in fermented/brewed drinks or to sweeten liqueurs and cocktails. Specialist brewing sugars are available, but we've always found white cane sugar works just fine. Darker sugars can also be used to add a different flavor to your drinks (and are specified in individual recipes), while other sweet ingredients, such as honey or maple syrup, can also be used in some recipes.

YEASTS

Our fermentable recipes will highlight the type of yeast to use, but in most instances these are recommendations, and not set in stone.

Wine yeast strains will enhance certain vinous qualities, while many beer and ale yeast strains have been cultivated to provide specific flavors to individual beer styles. It's best to go with the recommended yeasts if they are available, but even bread yeasts can be used if you are desperate. (These will tend to bring "bready" flavors to your drinks, which may or may not be a good thing; it's usually not.)

FINALLY, A WORD OF CAUTION

This book is about the easiest, most trouble-free, and fun route to some of the finest homemade drinks you could wish for. But be warned—there will be purists out there who might nit-pick over a few of our methods. Some craft beer advocates might insist you boil your beery mix for hours; wine connoisseurs may demand precise, temperature-controlled storing conditions for your bottles of wine; and certain "traditionalist" sections of the hard cider-making fraternity may consider the addition of other fruits and flavors to cider a terrible sin. If you like a drink style and want to get deeper under its skin or turn it into a career, by all means seek out more specialist advice. But if you want to arm yourself with a range of simple brewing techniques, impress your friends with your alcoholic output and have a load of stress-free fun on the way . . . read on.

HOW TO USE A HYDROMETER

A vital part of the home brewer's arsenal, the hydrometer will indicate the approximate sugar content in your drink, from which you can calculate the approximate amount of alcohol by volume (ABV) that resides in your fermented/brewed booze.

Hydrometers display "degrees of gravity" and are calibrated to read 1.000 in water, with the number increasing as the sugar content increases. Typically, ⅝ oz of sugar dissolved in 4½ cups of water will give a gravity reading of 1.010.

To take a reading, fill a measuring jar or tall glass with the liquid you wish to test. Clean the hydrometer, then drop it into the liquid, giving it a few spins to ensure that no bubbles cling to the stem, which might affect your calculation.

Look at the surface of the liquid and take a reading of where the liquid sits on the scale. To check the estimated alcohol content of your brew, you will need to take a reading before any yeast is added (starting gravity or original gravity) and after fermentation (final gravity). Note down the numbers, then subtract the finished gravity from the starting gravity and divide the result by 7.45.

For instance, we pressed Kingston Black/Michelin apple juice, which had an initial gravity of 1.070. We used this juice to make a splendid farmhouse hard cider (see page 52), which we allowed to fully ferment. We then took a reading, which told us the fermented juice had a finished gravity of 1.000.

- 1,070 minus 1,000 equals 70
- 70 divided by 7.45 equals 9.39
- Or, 9.4% alcohol by volume

This also told us not to drink too many of these ciders in one sitting!

If math was never your strong suit, fear not. The Internet is home to many free applications and websites that will do this calculation for you.

WINE & MEAD BASICS

Making homemade wine is a rewarding experience—the simple act of turning homegrown ingredients into alcohol through the miracle of science and nature is a beautiful thing.

There can be few things as hypnotic as a stream of bubbles rising through an airlock. You know that with each "plop" of gas, another drop of alcohol has been produced and your homemade wine is one step closer to being ready. However, the science is rarely exact, and nature is unpredictable, so you can never be too certain quite how your wine will turn out. But we consider that unpredictability one of the additional joys of wine making.

We've selected the wines in this book because they're relatively easy to make, use ingredients that you can grow, forage or easily source, and have all been tested and enjoyed by us. But given that each ingredient contains its own variable qualities (no one piece of fruit is exactly the same as the next), which further adds to the unpredictability of the process, don't get too obsessesive over exact weights and quantities—treat these recipes as a guide for your own adventures in wine making.

THE FERMENTATION PROCESS

Fermentation is simple: it's a process of turning a carbohydrate, such as sugar, into an acid or—in our case—alcohol and carbon dioxide. The latter is allowed to escape while the alcohol remains in the liquid. In wine making this boozy process is activated by adding yeast to a sugary liquid—the more sugar is used, the stronger the resulting alcoholic drink. From there it's down to your choice of edible ingredient to provide the flavor.

In this section we have also included a few mead recipes—these are ancient beverages that simply use honey as a source of sugar. As the honey contributes its own flavor, other ingredients are used to complement the honey notes rather than be a dominating presence. (See page 43 for more information on honey as an ingredient in wine making.)

WHAT MAKES A GOOD WINE?

People don't tend to wax lyrical about country wines nearly as much as they do about wines made from grapes. There aren't thousands of experts enthusing over why one vintage of pineapple is better than another, or whether each variety of rhubarb is in or out of fashion. So how do we know if our wines will be any good? For starters, it's important to emphasize that we're not trying to recreate wines with familiar grape flavors—elderberries will taste of elderberries, not Shiraz grapes—and some wines will have much less "vinous" qualities than others. So throw your preconceptions out of the window and treat each wine as a new flavor experience . . . if you enjoy the resulting beverage, then it's officially good!

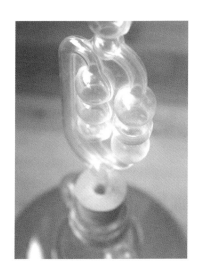

Having said this though, in general terms, a wine considered "good" by more critical tasters tends to have a balance of the following elements:

Acidity: Besides balancing the overall taste of wine, acids help the yeast with the important act of fermentation. For ingredients that are lacking in acid, lemons or powdered citric acid are useful additions.

Tannin: Another acid that is more prominent in red wines, giving drinks their rich, dry "mouthfeel"; tannin also helps protect the wine while it is aging. Tea contains tannin and can be used to give these qualities to homemade wines—Rich tends to favor black tea, while Nick prefers green tea in his recipes.

Body: This describes how full the flavor is and how punchy the wine tastes—wines said to be lacking in body will taste thin and light. If you prefer a meatier taste, body can be enhanced with the addition of fruit—we tend to favor golden raisins or raisins, but you can also use other dried fruits, grape juice concentrate or even bananas.

MAKER'S NOTES: YEAST

Specialist yeasts are available to help specific wines to perform better—but as these tend to be designed for grape varieties, we choose from three basic types of yeast: red wine, white wine and champagne. The first two are self-explanatory, but the latter is used for wines with high levels of sugar, as it survives through higher levels of alcohol. We buy dry yeast in individual sachets for ease of use. If you prefer to buy in bulk, around ⅛ ounces is a suitable quantity to add, but always refer to the instructions on the packet before using.

We also use yeast nutrient, which is a substance that helps to feed the yeast during the fermentation process to keep up its performance.

One of the main reasons why grapes have become the most-used wine ingredient is that they contain varying levels of all the above elements, as well as enough water and sugar to complete the job. It's the only one-stop-shop fruit out there, which is why our recipes require the addition of water, sugar and, in some cases, other supplementary ingredients. Of course, you can create perfectly drinkable wines with more or less of each of these qualities—taste is, after all, personal—so if you find yourself enjoying a wine packed with "body," work out what ingredients have provided this for one wine and use them in your next recipe.

THE BASIC PROCESS

Get a feel for the key steps involved in making wine, and you'll soon be devising your own recipes.

1. Extract flavors and sugars from the raw ingredients. Depending on what fruit or veg you're using this can be achieved in a number of ways, such as boiling, steeping or pressing.

2. Add water, sugar and any supplementary ingredients.

3. Start the initial rapid fermentation by adding yeast. This is usually done in a food-grade bucket, and sometimes "on the

pulp" (i.e. with the fruit still present to maximize flavor and sugar extraction).

4. Strain the liquid into a carboy for a slower, longer fermentation under the safety of an airlock.

5. After around one month, rack off wine to remove it from the mucky deposits known as the "lees" (see page 16).

6. Leave the wine for a few more months before bottling and maturing.

WHAT KIT DO I NEED?

The archetypal image of home wine making is the **carboy**. Traditionally glass, but also available in plastic, these vessels contain the liquid and are where most fermentation happens. They're fairly inexpensive and are a common feature of thrift stores and garage sales. We use a 1.1-gallon carboy. Other key items are as follows . . .

Airlock: A twisty tube (or more modern two-piece airlock) that is partially filled with sterilized water (preboiled, for example), allowing gas to escape without nasties entering your wine.

Bung: A rubber stopper with a hole running through it to connect the airlock to the carboy.

Fermenting bin: Any food-grade bucket will do, ideally with a lid. If there is no lid, use a dish towel or a piece of foil as a cover.

Big pot: Suitable for heating water and other ingredients.

Spoon: For stirring—if you can get one with a long, thin handle, it can be useful for stirring inside the carboy.

Plastic tube: For siphoning liquid from one carboy to another and, eventually, into bottles.

Corking device: Essential if you're plugging your bottles with corks (see page 17).

Muslin cloth or a fine sieve: To strain the liquid from the pulp.

Other useful but not essential tools include a cooking thermometer (to judge the yeast pitching temperature) and a hydrometer for measuring the wine's gravity which, in turn, tells you its alcoholic strength (see page 11).

C.J.J. BERRY

Back in 1960, amateur winemakers got their bible when C. J. J. Berry published *First Steps in Winemaking*. The book, containing 150 easy-to-follow recipes, is owned by over 3 million people and has inspired many wine-making enterprises. Besides documenting centuries-old country wine recipes, Berry also tackled unusual ingredients, and his measurements act as a starting point for thousands of subsequent recipes, including some of ours. Many of his creations are heavy on sugar, producing strong, sweet wines (we sometimes tone down the sugar for lighter tipples), and in his subsequent book *130 New Winemaking Recipes*, we sense he started running out of sensible ingredients—we have no desire to try his recipe for onion wine . . .

MAKER'S NOTES: HOW STRONG IS MY WINE?

We don't provide alcohol content estimations in our recipes, because there are too many variables involved for accurate predictions. If you wish to find out how much alcohol your wine contains, you'll need to learn how to use a hydrometer (it's easy, and instructions can be found in this book—see page 11). As a rough guide our wines will range from around 8 to 14 percent.

BEST FERMENTING CONDITIONS

Ideally, a wine needs to ferment at a steady temperature of 65 to 75°F. What it dislikes most is wild fluctuations of temperature (such as those it might be subjected to on a windowsill), so keep your carboy somewhere steadily warm. Heat pads and straps are available to help if your house doesn't naturally offer such a location. Direct sunlight is also to be avoided (another minus point for the windowsill), not least because this can strip the drink of its distinctive color.

The length of time it takes to ferment wine can vary according to ingredients, yeast quality and fermenting conditions. If you think your wine looks sluggish, the first racking often kick-starts it back into active fermentation. As a guide, we find that 3 months should be the minimum you need to keep your wine in a carboy before bottling. However, keeping it in the carboy for longer is no bad thing (it likes to mature in volume), provided you've racked it off from any sediment.

RACKING

"Racking" is the process of transferring your wine from one carboy to another, leaving behind the buildup of mucky sediment (the lees). We usually rack after around 1 month, when fermentation has significantly subsided or stopped altogether. A wine left too long on the lees is likely to pick up unwanted flavors. Racking also has the benefit of awakening sluggish yeast to finish the job of fermentation, and will start to bring a bit of clarity to the liquid. Some wines may need racking a second or even a third time at monthly intervals if there's a subsequent buildup of lees.

To rack your wine simply put a clean, sterilized carboy at a lower level than the wine-filled carboy and transfer the wine through a siphoning tube. You'll have to suck the end to get the wine flowing, which will give you a first taste of the immature liquid—don't be alarmed if it's not especially pleasant at this stage! As you near the lees, carefully tip the carboy containing the wine to get as much good liquid out before hitting the bad stuff (but don't worry if a drizzle of lees runs through the tube—you can rack again at a later stage).

If you've left behind a lot of lees, the new carboy will be less than full. Air and wine don't mix well, so you're best off topping this gap up. The simplest way is to use preboiled and cooled water, but bear in mind that this will slightly dilute the flavor and strength of the finished wine. To keep your wine at its predicted alcohol volume, dissolve sugar into the topping-up water—

MAKER'S NOTES: HOW LONG SHOULD I WAIT BEFORE DRINKING?

Drink your wine when it tastes nice enough to your own palate! Rich will often pop a cork months before the recommended maturation time—a young wine holds no fear for his taste buds—whereas Nick prefers to be patient and is known to wait for years before deploying the corkscrew. It tends to be the case that paler, less heavy wines are drinkable before darker drinks, but there are no hard rules. And you'll be surprised at how harsh or undesirable flavors in a young wine—with tannin being a common culprit for causing these—can mellow over time. Tannins are also responsible for allowing a wine to age successfully, so those light, tannin-free wines shouldn't be kept for long.

check the recipe to work out a rough weight of sugar per gallon and divide accordingly for your requirements. (Or, do as we do: guess.) A third option is to fill the space with something solid that won't affect the flavor—for this we use clear glass marbles, which have of course been sterilized before they enter the wine.

BOTTLING

It's hard to avoid spillage when siphoning wine from carboy to bottle, so put your empties on a towel or in a bucket as close to each other as you can. Our recipes will fill six standard 75 cl bottles (often with half a glass left over to sample). Although you can use screw caps, we recommend you don't—unless you're 100 percent certain all the yeast is no longer active a further fermentation may start in the bottles. This could lead to a buildup of pressure and, eventually, an explosion—so cork them up instead. You can either use traditional corks, or specially designed plastic stoppers which bung up the hole with a firm thrust of the palm. Don't think you have to discard any recycled screw-cap wine bottles, though—corks fit in these just fine.

STERILIZE!
As with all fermented drinks, make sure you sterilize every piece of equipment used at all stages of the process.

CHEMICAL AIDS

The fermentation process can be as natural as you want, but there are some chemicals you can use to help perfect your wine making.

Campden tablets: Added at least 24 hours before the yeast, Campden tablets sterilize raw ingredients and dispose of unwanted wild yeasts. They also ward off oxidation at bottling time. They're made up of sulfites, which some people have an allergy to, but fortunately their use is optional—use them if you want the added security of protecting your wine from nature's nasties.

Potassium sorbate: Can be added with a Campden tablet prior to bottling to kill off any lingering yeast, thus preventing further fermentation in the bottle (which can lead to prematurely popping corks and fizzy booze).

Pectic enzyme: Added to the pulp, this helps to reduce the chances of your wine going cloudy as a result of "pectin haze," and improves the juice yield.

Sweeteners: If you prefer your wines sweet (we think many fruit wines benefit from a touch of sugar), the easiest way to achieve this is to use an artificial sweetener. Homebrew stores sell sweeteners specifically produced for wine.

Citric acid: Used to give acidity to wine.

Making time: 45 minutes | **Fermenting time**: 3 months | **Maturing time**: 6 months

RHUBARB WINE

Rhubarb wine was the first drink we made from an allotment harvest, and it's a great starting wine for anyone: easy to make, uses a minimum of ingredients, and after a month of pie making you'll be desperate to put your rhubarb to some other culinary use. This recipe is adapted from C. J. J. Berry and produces consistently delicious results.

10 to 12 good-sized rhubarb sticks
(around 11 cups when diced)—
we prefer the larger, green stalks,
but pink ones will make your
wine look more like a rosé
5⅔ cups white sugar
1 teaspoon pectic enzyme
2 Campden tablets
white wine yeast
1 teaspoon yeast nutrient

MAKER'S NOTES: THE GREAT BLENDER

Some people make rhubarb wine for the sole purpose of blending it with other country wines. In flavor terms it tends to defer to other fruits, while adding more complexity to the finished tipple. For this reason it can also be mixed with different ingredients at the start of the process. Try experimenting with rhubarb and soft fruit combinations, or use it to give body to flower wines.

1. Clean and roughly chop the rhubarb sticks, put them in a sterilized food-grade bucket and hit them with a rolling pin so they break up. Add the sugar, pectic enzyme and a crushed Campden tablet and mix everything together. Cover and set aside overnight.

2. The next day the juice will have seeped out of the rhubarb to create a sticky syrup. Add to this 9 cups boiling water, and let cool.

3. Attach a funnel to the neck of a carboy and strain the juice through it using a fine sieve or muslin cloth. Press hard to remove as much liquid as possible.

4. Fill the carboy with around 9 cups preboiled, cooled water, leaving a shortfall of 1 to 2 inches to prevent the fermenting liquid from overflowing. Add the yeast and yeast nutrient, fit an airlock and keep the carboy in a warm place. After 1 week top up the carboy, again using preboiled water.

5. Continue to ferment until bubbling has all but ceased— 1 month should be long enough—then "rack off" the wine by siphoning it into a clean carboy, leaving behind any sediment.

6. If there's a shortfall in the new carboy, top this up with cool, preboiled water and refit the airlock. Leave it in a warm place another few months and if you're certain there's no more fermentation, stir in another crushed Campden tablet and siphon into bottles.

7. If you're desperate to sample your wares early, rhubarb is one of the few wines that can be cracked open 4 to 5 months after bottling with reasonable reward. Leave it alone for 9 months and any early acidic harshness should have mellowed, treating you to homemade wine perfection.

Making_time: 45 minutes | **Fermenting time**: 4 to 5 months | **Maturing time**: 9 months

ELDERBERRY WINE

It shouldn't be surprising that a berry known as "the English grape" produces one of the best red wines around. The rich red juices and tannins create a robust, spicy wine that tastes every bit as good as commercial wines. Some recipes use vast amounts of berries and take years to mature, but if you carefully follow our recipe then you should be drinking your wine sooner than most, and you'll also be left with berries that can be used again for a second-run wine (see page 22).

6¼ cups ripe elderberries
5⅔ cups white sugar
juice of 1 lemon
1 teaspoon pectic enzyme
2 Campden tablets
red wine yeast
1 teaspoon yeast nutrient

1. To detach the elderberries from their stalks we suggest flicking them off through the prongs of a fork. Try to avoid getting under- or overripe berries and green stems into the mix, although some of the thinner bits will inevitably slip through.

2. Put the berries into a food-grade bucket and add 4¾ cups boiling water. Cover with a lid and soak 24 hours.

3. Roughly press the berries with a rolling pin, a potato masher, or a clean pair of hands. Add the sugar and top up with another 10 cups boiling water. Stir to dissolve the sugar.

4. Let cool, then strain the liquid into a carboy through a muslin cloth or fine sieve. Add the lemon juice, pectic enzyme and 1 crushed Campden tablet, then stir the liquid.

5. Set aside another 24 hours before adding the yeast and yeast nutrient. Fit an airlock and put the carboy somewhere warm. There should be a shortfall of wine in the carboy—this is because it will start fermenting at a vigorous pace and overfilling will cause sticky red eruptions.

6. After a week the vigorous fermentation should have eased and you can top up the carboy with water. (This should have been preboiled and allowed to cool first.)

7. Rack the wine into a clean carboy after around 1 month and leave another 3 to 4 months—after this time fermentation should be finished and the wine will be ready for bottling.

8. Stir 1 Campden tablet into the wine using a sterilized spoon, then siphon it into bottles. Allow the wine to mature at least 9 months before drinking.

NICK'S TIP:
SQUEEZY DOES IT
Be gentle when straining the juice
into your carboy. Press through
as much juice as you can without
squeezing too hard—overexertion will
cause too much tannin to escape
from the skins, resulting in a
mustier wine that will take
longer to mature.

Making time: 40 minutes | **Fermenting time**: 3 months | **Maturing time**: 9 months

SECOND-RUN ELDERBERRY & PLUM WINE

The practice of making "second-run" wines from grapes that have already been pressed is fairly common, and the same thrifty trick can be applied to used elderberries. After making your initial wine there'll be enough elderberry goodness for another batch, offering you the opportunity to introduce another ingredient to boost the flavor. Plums make a perfect companion to elderberries—and you can use whatever type you wish; we've had most success with a mix of damsons, sloes, and bullaces.

the elderberries left over from Elderberry Wine (see page 20)
1⅛ pounds damsons, sloes or bullaces, prepared as described in Step 2
2 Campden tablets
1 teaspoon pectic enzyme
juice and zest of 1 unwaxed lemon
5⅔ cups white sugar
red wine yeast
yeast nutrient

1. Salvage your pressed elderberries and put them into a clean, sterilized food-grade bucket.

2. Wash your plums. If they're large and it's easy to remove the stones, then do so. If you're using damsons, sloes or bullaces, slash the skins with a knife and leave the stones in. Put the fruit into the bucket with the elderberries.

3. Add 1 crushed Campden tablet, the pectic enzyme and the lemon juice and zest. Pour over 4¾ cups boiling water, cover and set aside for 24 hours.

4. Give the fruit a bash with a rolling pin or potato masher, or squeeze it with your hands. If your plums still contain stones, be careful not to break them.

5. Add the sugar and pour in another 13½ cups boiling water. Stir to dissolve the sugar, then set aside to cool.

6. Once cooled, add the yeast and yeast nutrient. Cover with a loose-fitting lid and ferment in a warm spot 5 to 6 days, stirring daily with a sterilized spoon.

7. Strain the bubbling liquid into a carboy, topping up with preboiled water if there's a shortfall, and fit an airlock.

8. Rack the wine after 1 month and ferment to a finish a further 2 months, racking again if more sediment builds up.

9. Before bottling, carefully stir another crushed Campden tablet into the wine. Siphon into bottles and store for a minimum of 9 months before opening.

MAKER'S NOTES: AN ALTERNATIVE TO PLUMS

You don't have to add stone fruit such as plums to a second pressing of elderberries. Other choices include blackberries, cherries, raspberries or, obviously, more elderberries. We've even seen recipes for the unusual-sounding combination of elderberry and green bean wine, but have yet to try this option ourselves.

Making time: 40 minutes | **Fermenting time**: 3 months | **Maturing time**: 9 months

ELDERFLOWER WINE

No flowers have quite matched the culinary acceptance of the elderflower. It's becoming an increasingly common flavor for drinks on grocery store shelves, and you'll often find it used in desserts as people become more adventurous with their foraging. The flowers' heady aroma makes them a perfect choice for the home winemaker—wines such as Sauvignon Blanc are often compared to elderflower, so why not use the real thing? You can make a perfectly acceptable light wine without including other flavors, but we think this recipe is a good choice to start you off experimenting with adding more fruit to create a richer, more complex—and boozier—tipple.

15 to 20 elderflower heads*
  (depending on size and
  thoroughness of flower removal)
juice and zest of 3 unwaxed
  lemons
5⅔ cups white sugar
1 mug of black or green tea
1 handful of dried fruit, chopped
  (see Step 2)
2 Campden tablets
1 teaspoon pectic enzyme
white wine yeast
yeast nutrient

1. Give the flower heads a shake and rinse to remove any bugs, before tearing off the flowers into a bucket. A few tiny bits of stalk will inevitably join them, but try to avoid too many large bits, as these will impart a bitter taste to the finished wine.

2. Add the juice and zest (avoiding the bitter pith) of the lemons, the sugar and the tea. You can add various kinds of chopped dried fruit—raisins and golden raisins are the most popular choices, but you could also use dried figs, dates or apricots. (We also throw in a chopped rhubarb stick if there's one to hand.) These will all give your wine body, and may also change the color of the liquid.

3. Add 1 Campden tablet at this point, along with 1 teaspoon of pectic enzyme.

4. Pour 18 cups boiling water into the bucket, stir thoroughly to dissolve the sugar, loosely cover with a lid, and set aside to cool overnight.

5. Add the yeast and yeast nutrient, cover again and leave 5 to 7 days, stirring the mixture each day.

6. Strain the wine into a carboy and fit an airlock. Rack off when bubbles stop rising (after around 1 month) and bottle 2 months later (adding another Campden tablet before doing so). Try to wait until the following year's elderflowers are in bloom before opening—early tastings are drinkable but lack the quality of a more mature wine.

*Always sniff elderflowers before picking. Some blooms have a smell reminiscent of cats' urine, and you don't want your wine to taste like cheap lager.

Making time: 1 hour | **Fermenting time**: 4 months | **Maturing time**: 6 to 12 months

CRAB APPLE WINE

The very mention of crab apple wine may lead to sideways glances from skeptical friends, but trust us, the often harsh acidity synonymous with the crab apple will mellow through fermentation and aging, resulting in a tannin-rich, tangy wine. Crab apples vary from tree to tree, ranging wildly from the gut-wrenchingly tart to those with a sweeter disposition, so write copious notes when making this wine and experiment with different blends to find your preferred fruity combination.

6 pounds crab apples
juice and zest of 1 unwaxed lemon
6¼ cups sugar
champagne yeast*
yeast nutrient
pectic enzyme
1 Campden tablet

1. When you pick the crab apples it's better to collect too many, as you can always use the surplus for jelly. (Ask your Grandma for a recipe.) Wash and chop the apples, discarding the ones that have been savaged by pests or are rotting.

2. Bring 9 cups water to a boil in a large pot or jam pan, then add the chopped apples, the lemon zest and the sugar. Stir the mixture, then simmer 20 minutes.

3. Strain the liquid into a fermentation bucket, leaving behind the cooked apple and lemon zest. Boil 9 cups water and add this to the mixture.

4. When the liquid has cooled to room temperature, add the yeast, yeast nutrient, pectic enzyme and lemon juice. Cover and leave to ferment 3 days.

5. Strain the mixture through a muslin cloth into a carboy, fit an airlock and continue to ferment the wine in a warm room until bubbling all but ceases, which should take 4 to 6 weeks.

6. Rack the wine into a clean carboy and leave for a further 2 months. Add a Campden tablet to the carboy before siphoning into bottles.

7. This wine should be ready after 6 months of maturing, but if you find the wine still too acidic at this stage, put it back in the cupboard for further maturing and crack open a hard cider instead.

This is adapted from one of C. J. J. Berry's recipes and is one of our favorites. Like many of his recipes, it uses a large mound of sugar, hence the need for champagne yeast, which will go the extra mile.

SCRUMPING NOTES

The small, camouflaged apples of the crab are not that easy to spot among the hedgerows in fall. It's advisable to do your detective work in spring, looking out for their telltale pinky-white blossoms and noting down the locations for foraging later in the year.

Making_time: 40 minutes | **Fermenting time**: 3 to 4 months | **Maturing time**: 6 months

FRAGRANT FIG WINE

There will come a time when the urge to ferment coincides with a lack of natural ingredients to hand—in which case, try this exotic treat made entirely out of dried ingredients. You can stock up on figs from most grocery stores or health food stores, while rose petals are a cheap staple of homebrew suppliers. This combination of North African-inspired ingredients is an olfactory sensation, and makes a highly desirable wine.

1½ cups dried rose petals
6 cups dried figs,
   finely chopped
2½ pounds/5¼ cups/1.15 kg
   sugar
juice and zest of 1 unwaxed lemon
1 teaspoon pectic enzyme
white wine yeast
1 teaspoon yeast nutrient
2 Campden tablets

1. Put the dried rose petals into a large cooking pot (tie them into a muslin bag if you have one). Add 9 cups water, bring to a boil and simmer 15 minutes.

2. Meanwhile, chop the figs—if you don't want to take the time-consuming approach of using a sharp-bladed knife, try pulverizing them in a mincer or electric dicing machine. Put the figgy pieces into a food-grade bucket with the sugar, lemon juice, pared lemon zest (make sure there is no pith), the pectic enzyme and a crushed Campden tablet.

3. When the rose petals have finished their simmer, strain them through muslin into the bucket. Boil a further 9 cups water and add to the mix, stirring to dissolve the sugar.

4. Cover the bucket and set aside for 24 hours before adding the yeast and yeast nutrient. Stir the mixture, put the cover back on and put it somewhere warm. Continue to stir every day for 6 to 7 days.

5. After this time strain the liquid into a clean carboy, topping up with cool, preboiled water if necessary, and fit an airlock. Return to your warm location and keep out of direct sunlight to preserve the color. After around 1 month, when fermentation has subsided, rack the wine into another carboy.

6. Keep the wine in the carboy for another 2 to 3 months and, when you're certain fermentation has ceased, gently stir 1 Campden tablet into the wine using a sterilized spoon, before siphoning it into bottles.

7. We've found that this wine is drinkable when surprisingly young—just 4 months after bottling—but we recommend waiting for a minimum of 6 months.

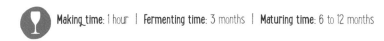

Making time: 1 hour | **Fermenting time**: 3 months | **Maturing time**: 6 to 12 months

PINEAPPLE WINE

Sadly we are never going to experience the joy of harvesting plump pineapples from our damp, windswept allotment plot, but we would heartily recommend a trip to your local grocery store to "forage" a couple of prickly fruits to make this tropical treat of a wine. It's one of those rare homemade wines that maintains its fruity flavors during fermentation, right through to the finished glass. Time to don your grass skirt—it's a Hawaiian* hula-dance in a bottle.

2 pineapples
6¼ cups sugar
juice of 1 lemon
1 cup of black or green tea
champagne yeast
yeast nutrient
pectic enzyme
1 Campden tablet

1. Top and tail the pineapples, then slice and dice them into cubes.

2. Bring 9 cups water to a boil in a large pot or jam pan, add the diced pineapple and simmer 25 minutes.

3. Meanwhile, tip the sugar, lemon juice, tea (for tannin) and 9 cups water into a sterilized fermenting bin.

4. Strain the stewed pineapples through a muslin cloth into the fermenting bin and stir.

5. When cool, add the champagne yeast, nutrient, and pectic enzyme, then cover and leave in a warm place about 1 week.

6. Fermentation should now be under way, so transfer to a 4¾-quart carboy and fit an airlock.

7. When the airlock no longer bubbles (after around 1 month), rack the wine into another clean carboy and wait a further 2 months. Add 1 Campden tablet to the carboy before siphoning the wine into bottles.

8. This fruity little number will benefit from maturing, so leave 6 months or up to 1 year before enjoying.

SERVING SUGGESTIONS

Make a summery spritzer with a 50/50 mix of wine and sparkling water, or you can use lemonade for an extra fizzy treat, then top it off with a slice of fresh pineapple and a paper umbrella for a touch of class.

Although Hawaii is the spiritual home of commercial pineapple plantations, Christopher Columbus first introduced them to Europe (and then the South Sea Islands) from Guadeloupe in 1493. In return he gave them rats, lettuce and malaria . . .

GOING BANANAS FOR ANANAS
Pineapples are known as ananas in many countries. This is derived from the Tupian word *nanas*, meaning "excellent fruit."
FACT!

GRAPEFRUIT WINE

This wine is a celebration of the grapefruit—the fat, yellow (and sometimes pink) globe that is rarely eaten after breakfast. We're such fans of the grapefruit that we're happy to show it off unadulterated with any other fruits in all its citrussy glory. If you want a crisp, light wine that's easy to make, then raise a glass to the grapefruit.

4½ cups sugar
5 large grapefruit, scrubbed, zest thinly pared from 2 of them
2 Campden tablets
white wine yeast
yeast nutrient
1 teaspoon pectic enzyme

1. Put the sugar into a clean, sterilized fermentation bucket. Boil 4 cups water and pour over the sugar, stirring to dissolve.

2. Pour 13½ cups cold water into the bucket (bringing the total water volume up to 18 cups).

3. Put the zest from two of the grapefruit into the bucket. Make sure to avoid the pith, as it will make the drink bitter.

4. Squeeze the juice from all five grapefruit into the bucket, and to this sweet citrussy liquid add a crushed Campden tablet.

5. Cover the bucket with a lid or clean dish towel and let cool 24 hours, then add the yeast, yeast nutrient,and pectic enzyme. Leave to ferment 3 days.

6. Strain the mixture through a fine sieve or muslin cloth into a carboy, fit an airlock and continue to ferment in a warm room around 1 month.

7. Rack the wine into a clean carboy. After a few weeks it's likely that another fair-sized layer of sediment will have settled. If this is the case, rack the wine for a second time.

8. When the wine has finished fermenting—around 2 months after first racking—add a crushed Campden tablet to the carboy before siphoning into bottles. Set aside at least 6 months, and preferably 1 year, before drinking.

Making time: 1 hour | **Fermenting time:** 3 months | **Maturing time:** 12 months

LEMON & LIME WINE

Evoke the scents of a Tuscan hilltop stroll (or a shuffle through a grocery store's fruit aisle) with this classic citrus combination. It's bright, crisp, zest-fest and a cut above your average plonk. It will, however, benefit from a slightly longer maturation time to round out those sharp, citrus notes. Ferment, bottle . . . and be patient.

juice and zest of 4 unwaxed lemons
juice and zest of 4 unwaxed limes
6¼ cups sugar
1 handful of chopped raisins
1 cup of strong black tea
white wine yeast
yeast nutrient
pectic enzyme
1 Campden tablet

1. Put the lemon and lime zest in a sterilized fermenting bin. Take care not to include too much white pith, as this will result in unwanted bitterness.

2. Add the lemon and lime juice to the fermenting bin.

3. Add the sugar, raisins and tea, and stir the mixture.

4. Boil 18 cups water in a separate pan, then add to the fermenting bin, give it a good stir and let cool.

5. Add the yeast, yeast nutrient and pectic enzyme, then cover the fermenting bin with a lid or dish towel and leave in a warm place about 1 week.

6. By now, fermentation should be under way, so strain the mixture through a muslin cloth into a carboy and fit an airlock.

7. After about 1 month fermentation should have subsided, so rack into another sterilized carboy and continue to ferment to completion—this will take a further 2 months or so.

8. Add 1 Campden tablet to the carboy before siphoning into bottles, corking and stowing the wine away to mature.

MAKER'S NOTES: PHYTOPHOTODERMATITIS

A common affliction affecting cocktail-making bartenders, phytophotodermatitis (try saying that with a mouthful of chips) is where skin in prolonged contact with certain fruits and plants becomes hypersensitive to sunlight and starts to burn. While this is particularly prevalent among those handling lemons and limes, other plants that contain the blistering chemical compounds include carrots, celery, parsley and parsnips. Now wash your hands.

 **Making time**: 1 hour | **Fermenting time**: 3 months | **Maturing time**: 12 months

PARSNIP WINE

Parsnip wine is one of the finest drinks a home brewer can make, and is also one of the most popular, as visits to our website demonstrate. The inherent rooty spiciness of this wine lends itself to experimentation and adaptation; our annual glut of allotment parsnips allow us this luxury, and provide the ammunition for an ever-escalating "wine war," where we do battle with our recipes to see who can produce the most sippable parsnips. Now behold Rich's all-conquering recipe of champions . . .

4 pounds parsnips, scrubbed
    and chopped
6¼ cups sugar
juice and zest of 2 unwaxed
    lemons
juice and zest of 1 orange
white wine yeast
yeast nutrient
pectic enzyme
1 Campden tablet

1. Toss your parsnips into a large pan along with 18 cups water (or as much as your pan can hold), then add the sugar and the lemon and orange juice and zest.

2. Bring gently to a boil, then continue to heat until the parsnips become soft. Don't overboil, or your parsnips will start to disintegrate, and this will result in a cloudy wine.

3. Let cool, then strain the liquid through a muslin cloth into a fermenting bin. Add the yeast, yeast nutrient and pectic enzyme, then cover with a dish towel and leave in a warm place around 5 days.

4. Strain the now-fermenting liquid into a carboy and fit an airlock.

5. After about 4 weeks fermentation should have subsided, so you can rack the liquid into another sterilized carboy and continue to ferment to completion—usually around a further 2 months.

6. Add 1 Campden tablet to the carboy before siphoning the wine into bottles, corking and leaving to mature at least 1 year.

RICH'S TIP
If you want to follow centuries of wisdom, pick your parsnips after they have been hit by frost, and scrub them rather than peel. Frost signals the creation of natural sugars, which, along with the flavor, are more concentrated just beneath the surface.

SERVING SUGGESTIONS
Parsnip chips make a superb accompaniment when quaffing parsnip wine. To make them, simply shave off slivers of parsnip using a potato peeler and put them on a baking sheet. Brush the slivers with olive oil, add a sprinkle or two of salt, then bake in a preheated oven at 350°F 10 minutes.

🥄 ROOTS

They may not seem like the most obvious contenders for brew-it-yourself endeavors, but root vegetables come packed with that most important of alcohol-making substances: sugar. And with brewable roots ranging from veg box staples to bizarre botanicals, these underground ingredients can be used in a wider variety of drinks than you might think.

ROOTS IN BOOZE

The most commonly used root vegetables in our recipes barely get a mention in this book: sugar beet and the humble potato may be somewhat anonymous, but their presence is far-reaching. Around 20 percent of the world's sugar is extracted from the bulbous burrower sugar beet, while potatoes are a common ingredient in vodka. But we neither manufacture sugar nor distil spirits, so the most likely boozy use for a raw root in our kitchens will be as the base for a country wine or the flavoring for any number of craft drinks. Ginger receives the most credits in our recipes (Rich especially is a ginger addict, and uses it for a touch of heat in just about anything); dandelion roots make for a refreshing, light beer; and carrots, parsnips and beets can all be made into decent country wines. We've also seen recipes for wines made from potatoes, turnips and even onions—but all reports suggest they taste as bad as they sound.

USING ROOTS

Carrots, parsnips and beets are all easy to grow in large quantities, making the plot-to-bottle journey particularly rewarding for the home brewer. And by growing your own you get to experiment with varieties not so commonly available in the stores, from Purple Haze carrots to stripy Chioggia beets. If you're using roots to ferment with, veg harvested after a few frosts will contain the most sugar. The majority of this sugar and flavor is concentrated just beneath the surface, making scrubbing preferable to peeling. Botanical roots, used to flavor wines and spirits (see opposite), are less likely to be homegrown. So, if you're looking for an unusual rooty ingredient to make your drinks stand out from the crowd, you'll probably have to source it dried or as flavored extracts from a herbalist or online specialist.

DIG THIS!
MORE UNUSUAL BOOZY ROOTS

Horseradish: Makes for a particularly powerful vodka flavoring, and can add some oomph to a bloody Mary.

Mangelwurzel: This magnificently monikered veg is grown mainly for cattle, but there were times when country folk would turn it into beer or wine.

Dandelion and burdock: This famous double-act is made from the roots of both weeds. An alcoholic version of this drink is recommended.

Skirret (pictured): A relative of the parsnip, it has been suggested that this little-known perennial veg was one of the first flavorings used in beer.

Liquorice and other botanicals: Its strong aniseed flavor makes liquorice one of a number of rooty botanicals used to flavor alcohol. Other less-familiar ingredients include gentian root (used for bitterness in vermouths and bitters), sassafras (the original root beer flavor) and angelica (imparts a pungent herby flavor akin to juniper).

MINT WINE

When growth in the garden is abundant and we're in the brewing groove, we'll sometimes grab any random foodstuff and turn it into wine—more in hope than expectation. The concoction featuring pea and bean pods isn't worth repeating, but one of our surprising successes is this minty creation. The dried fruit provides a strong, vinous body while the mint gives it a crisp freshness and pleasant, tingly finish. Served ice cold it has become a barbecue favorite, and also makes a super spritzer diluted with soda water or lemonade.

4 cups fresh mint leaves stripped
   from the stalks
5½ cups sugar
2 Campden tablets
½ mug of black or green tea
1 handful of golden raisins, or
   other dried fruit (such as raisins,
   figs or apricots), chopped
juice of 2 lemons
white wine yeast
yeast nutrient

1. Rinse the mint leaves, and boil in 9 cups water around 10 minutes.

2. While the liquid is boiling, put the sugar, 1 crushed Campden tablet, the black or green tea and the golden raisins into a fermenting bucket.

3. After boiling, strain the hot minty liquid into the bucket and return the soggy leaves to the pan—use these again in a second 10-minute boil with another 9 cups water.

4. Strain this new batch of water into the bucket and stir to dissolve the sugar.

5. Cover the bucket with a lid or clean dish towel and let cool overnight. The following morning, put the lemon juice in the bucket and then add the yeast and yeast nutrient. Put the bucket in a warm place and leave to ferment 3 to 5 days.

6. Strain the mixture into a carboy, fit an airlock and continue to ferment in a warm room for around 1 month.

7. Rack the wine into a clean carboy and allow it to ferment out—an additional 2 to 3 months should be fine. When the wine has finished fermenting, add 1 crushed Campden tablet to the carboy before siphoning the wine into bottles.

8. Your wine should be drinkable after 6 months.

NICK'S TIP
COOKING WINE
It may seem rude to even consider using your homemade wine to cook with, but it really can give dishes a distinctive lift in place of regular grape wine. Mint wine, for example, works well in fresh pea, spinach or nettle risotto.

Making time: 1 hour | **Fermenting time**: 3 months | **Maturing time**: 6 months

OAK LEAF WINE

Fans of oaky wines need look no farther, as there is none more oaky than this delicious, leafy little number. We've made versions of this wine with new leaves picked in spring and older leaves harvested just before the fall kicks in—their rich tannins build throughout the year so the more mature leaves will maximize the mouth-puckering tannic effect. The citrus fruits added to this wine help to balance out the tannins . . . without them the resulting wine would be the liquid equivalent of eating bark.

1 shopping bag full of oak leaves
6¼ cups sugar
juice and zest of 2 oranges
juice and zest of 2 unwaxed
    lemons
white wine yeast
yeast nutrient
1 Campden tablet

1. Wash the oak leaves to evict any pests that may be lurking within, then put them in a fermenting bucket or large saucepan.

2. Boil 19 cups water in a separate pan, and pour on to the leaves. Cover with a lid or dish towel and leave to marinate 24 hours.

3. Strain the liquid through a muslin cloth, then add the sugar. Give it a stir before adding the zest and juice of the oranges and lemons.

4. Bring the mixture to a boil, then simmer 20 minutes, taking care not to overboil.

5. Remove from heat and let cool before straining into a carboy. Add the white wine yeast and nutrient, fit an airlock then leave to ferment in a warm place.

6. Rack the wine into a clean carboy when fermentation slows (after around 4 to 6 weeks). Leave to ferment to a finish about 2 more months.

7. Add 1 Campden tablet to the carboy before bottling, and allow the wine to mature at least 6 months before getting oaky.

RICH'S TIP
GRUB'S UP

Oak leaves harbor many pests, but don't worry about spotting them all before proceeding. Once you've added the hot water, the offending critters will magically rise to the surface, boiled and bloated, making it easy to whisk them away with a slotted spoon.

Making time: 1 hour | **Fermenting time**: 4 months | **Maturing time**: 6 months

EASY MEAD

Its origins go way back in time, but the Welsh (known for their excellence in drinking) claim it their tipple of choice ever since the Romans first herded bees across the Severn Bridge circa AD 47.* Its notoriously long maturation period puts many people off, but the following recipe is a simple version and will have you supping this golden nectar sooner than most. If at all possible, you should try to source your own local honey from free-range bees for a better-quality drink. Failing that, any store-bought organic honey should do the trick.

3 pounds honey
1 apple, chopped
½ cup chopped raisins
juice of 1 lemon
champagne yeast
yeast nutrient
1 Campden tablet

1. Pour 4 cups water into a saucepan and add the honey. (You'll find that immersing honey pots in hot water for 5 minutes will make the honey easier to pour.)

2. Warm the mixture over low heat, and stir in the honey.

3. Foam will start to appear on the surface, so skim this off with a wooden spoon or similar utensil.

4. When no more foam rises, rejoice and remove from heat.

5. When your mixture has cooled sufficiently, pour it into a clean carboy and top up with 14 cups water.

6. Add the chopped apple and raisins and the lemon juice, then add the yeast and yeast nutrient and give the liquid a good shake.

7. Fit a loose cotton wool bung to keep any airborne nasties from spoiling your mead, and leave in a warm room 2 to 3 days to help build strong yeast cells.

8. When fermentation is under way, fit an airlock and put the carboy somewhere cool.

9. After 2 months, rack into another clean carboy (leaving behind the emaciated fruit) and leave to clear.

10. Wait another 2 months, then add a Campden tablet before bottling and maturing a further 6 months.

ODIN'S GOAT OF MANY COLORS
In Norse mythology, Odin was said to keep a pet goat called Heidrún, who grazed on the tree on the roof of Valhalla. When asked nicely, the goat would produce mead from her udders to quench the dead thirsty Vahallians below.

Completely unsubstantiated historical fact.

HONEY

Fermenting honey was primitive man's first attempt at booze making, and brewers have been harnessing its golden powers ever since, creating mead wines (its most well-known boozy manifestation) and using it to flavor beers, hard ciders, cocktails and spirits. Whatever drink you are planning to brew, you can be sure there's a place in it for honey.

FLOWER POWER

It's always best to source your honey as locally as possible, but this community-spirited approach may well limit your choice. For the small-time beekeeper, honey flavor is difficult to dictate, as it is largely determined by the flowers from which the bees gather nectar. This is less of a problem, of course, for the store-bound forager who can choose from a wide variety of styles.

Ultimately, your choice should be guided by the alcoholic concoction you want to make. Punchy flavors such as those of heather honey are great for wines and meads, while you may prefer the more subtle flavors provided by orange blossom honey when making a honey beer, or if you wish to add rich sweetness to a cocktail without drowning out the taste of other more delicate additions.

GO WITH THE FLOW

Honey consists mainly of fructose and glucose, the proportions of which determine the type of honey that is produced. Honey containing a high proportion of fructose will usually be runny and clear, while honey that has a high glucose percentage will tend to crystallize more readily. This has no bearing on flavor, but runny honey is more convenient for the home brewer as it leaves the jar easily, without a fight. To "runnify" a solid honey, simply warm it gently, taking care not to overheat it as this will have a detrimental effect on its floral notes.

IN FOR THE LONG HAUL

Mead and winemakers who would like to ferment with honey should take note—honey is surprisingly lacking in the nutrients required by yeast to start the fermentation process, so it's advisable to add yeast nutrient along with yeast to get things up and running. Once it starts, however, it'll take some stopping . . . honey has a notoriously long fermentation time, so be prepared for a wait.

FEED THE BEES

Turn your yard into a pollinator's paradise with our top five bee-attracting plants.

Dog rose: Produces beautiful wild blooms, and will also provide the fruit required for rosehip syrup in Rosehip Hard Cider (see page 62).

Rosemary: Bees and hoverflies will flock to this herb. Better still, you can borrow a sprig or two to liven up a dull gin and tonic.

Crab apple: The flowers of the varieties John Downie and Golden Hornet both come packed with pollen and nectar. Their tiny, tannic fruit is also used to bolstering thin hard ciders.

Sage: Its fragrant flowers are sure to please the bees, and you can also make a rather pungent, herby wine from the leaves (although we prefer to save our sage for stuffing roast chickens).

Yarrow: Bees go crazy for yellow yarrow, so give the vigorous Coronation Gold variety a go. Its stems and leaves can also be used as a bittering agent in beer making.

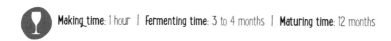

RHODOMEL (ROSEHIP MEAD)

The rose is a prickly beast of a plant that doesn't relinquish its fruit gladly, but scratched hands are a small price to pay for a foraged bag of the versatile, vitamin C-packed berries that will feed this mead. Marry your rosehips with a lightly flavored honey if you can, so as not to swamp the berries' subtle, fruity flavors.

1 pound rosehips
3 pounds honey
juice and zest of 1 unwaxed lemon
½ cup chopped raisins
champagne yeast
yeast nutrient
1 Campden tablet

1. Wash the rosehips, then mash them up with a mortar and pestle (or wrap them in a plastic bag/dish towel and hit with a rolling pin) then stuff them inside a muslin bag.

2. Put the bag in a saucepan along with 8 cups water, bring to a boil and simmer 20 minutes, skimming off any scum that rises. Remove from the heat and allow to infuse for 24 hours.

3. Strain the liquid and remove the muslin bag. Add honey to the hip-infused water, heat gently and stir until combined.

4. Add the juice and zest of the lemon, and the raisins; give everything a quick stir and transfer to a fermenting bucket.

5. Boil 10 cups water, add it to the fermenting bucket and let cool.

6. Add champagne yeast and nutrient, cover with a dish towel and leave 3 days.

7. Put a muslin cloth-lined funnel into the neck of a clean carboy and pour in the contents of your fermenting bucket. You may need to top up the carboy, so pour in cooled, preboiled water until the carboy is filled to the neck. Fit an airlock and leave to ferment.

8. After fermentation has ceased (about 2 months), rack the mead into a clean carboy.

9. Top up with water if necessary, refit an airlock, then leave the mead a further 1 to 2 months.

10. Add a Campden tablet before bottling, then leave the mead to mature at least 1 year before drinking. Hip hip hooray!

MAKER'S NOTES: GET DOMESTICATED

Hips from wild "dog" roses make the best meads and syrups, but you can also use domesticated varieties if you like. With its huge seed-bearing hips, the Rugosa rose is one of our favorites to plunder.

Making_time: 1 hour | Fermenting time: 3 to 4 months | Maturing time: 12 months

WINTER MEAD

Add herbs and spices to mead and you'll be making the ancient booze called metheglin. The imbibing of this style of mead was believed to have medicinal benefits, but who hasn't used that old excuse? We've used a cornucopia of Christmassy spices in our festively flavorsome version, along with some punchy allotment-sourced herbs for good measure. Just don't use it as a post-Christmas hangover cure.

3 tablespoons parsley
3 tablespoons lemon thyme
1 tablespoon sage
1 tablespoon rosemary
2-inch piece gingerroot, peeled
  and roughly chopped
10 cloves
1 cinnamon stick
3 pounds honey
champagne yeast
yeast nutrient
1 Campden tablet

1. Chop up the herbs, crunch up the spices and stuff them inside a muslin bag, ensuring they are wrapped up tightly enough to fit through the neck of a carboy.

2. Put the spice bag in a saucepan along with 8 cups water, bring to a boil and simmer for 15 minutes. Remove from the heat and allow the herbs to infuse 24 hours.

3. Strain then remove the herb bag, and set aside. Add the honey to the herb-infused water, then simmer and stir carefully until the water and honey have combined. Boil 9 cups water and add it to the mixture before leaving to cool.

4. Carefully pour the liquid into a carboy, add the muslin bag (or take it out of the trash if you weren't paying attention in Step 3), then add the champagne yeast and yeast nutrient.

5. Fit an airlock and await fermentation, which should commence after a couple of days and continue for around 2 months.

6. After fermentation has ceased, rack the mead into a clean carboy, leaving behind the muslin bag.

7. Top up with water, refit an airlock, then leave the mead a further 1 to 2 months.

8. Bottle when fermentation is complete, first adding a crushed Campden tablet to the carboy, then leave to mature at least 1 year before enjoying its powers of rejuvenation.

RICH'S TIP
BREW UP
This is a great recipe for experimenting with different ingredients, but you may want to make a black "tea" from your chosen herbs and spices to test the flavors before making the mead. There's no point wasting good honey!

HARD CIDER BASICS

Producing hard cider is as easy or as difficult as you wish to make it. On a basic level, leaving apple juice to ferment naturally in a bucket is pretty much all there is to it, but cider is a drink that deserves a more considered approach. Winemakers wouldn't dream of treating grapes in such a manner and, as cidermakers, nor should we. We've been making cider for years and are still experimenting with blends and techniques in the hope of making something extra-special, golden and glorious.

There are many variables with hard cider making (seasonal or otherwise) that will affect the finished drink, but the taste and style of your cider are largely defined by the blend of apples used, and this is where the artistry lies. When taking your first tentative steps in hard cider making, we suggest experimenting with small batches and making copious notes to aid you in future cidery endeavors.

WHAT APPLES CAN I USE?

You can use any apples to make hard cider—it really depends on what is available to you, and your personal taste. Chances are, the majority of your fruit will be dessert or culinary apples picked from back-yard trees in your local area. A juice blend of these types of apple will give you a German-style hard cider that will have clean, sharp characteristics. If you are lucky enough to have access to cider apples, and if all goes to plan, you will be able to produce a richer, fuller, tannin-rich hard cider known in the UK as "West Country" style.

PREPARING THE FRUIT

Give your apples a quick wash to remove any dirt, and discard any rotten fruit. Washing them before pressing is not entirely necessary, as pathogens cannot survive the alcohol levels in cider after fermentation. However, it's advisable not to drink the freshly squeezed juice during pressing, especially if your apples are collected from orchards where animals and livestock have been freely flinging their feces in joyful abandon.

MILLING THE APPLES

To maximize juice extraction you'll need to break down the apples prior to pressing. Wine makers have got it easy—grapes give out juices with the lightest touch of a Frenchman's toe—but apples require a bit more coaxing before they will part with theirs.

You'll need to crush your apples down to the consistency of thick oatmeal before squeezing, and there are various methods by which you can achieve this, depending on your budget and the number of apples you have to process. For example, there are many apple mills or "scratters" available to buy, ranging from small, hand-cranked mechanical ones to glorified garden shredders, specifically designed for dealing with juice-laden apples. However, for small batches of hard cider, using a wooden fencepost (or similar-sized piece of timber) to bash chopped up apples in a large tub makes a cheap and effective (if strenuous) option.

STERILIZE!

Purists, don't fret about adding sulfite. Traditional hard cidermakers used to burn sulfur candles in their cider barrels to sterilize them; this is just the modern way of doing it.

PRESSING

As with milling, there are various commercial options for pressing. We've used a small 2.6-gallon basket press for many years, and it has given us excellent service. Things start to get time-consuming when producing anything above 22 gallons, so if you ever find yourself approaching this volume (you will ... cider making is addictive!) you'll need to think bigger. Traditionally styled "rack and cloth" presses are more efficient with regard to the amount of juice they can extract, as the milled apples are wrapped in cloth and loaded onto the press between wooden or plastic layered slats. As the pressure is applied, each layer presses against each other, squeezing out the juice in a most efficient manner.

You can buy these types of presses (look for specialist companies online), or if you are feeling handy you could even try making one yourself. A homemade press can be assembled by building a strong frame out of wood or metal, with a tray or trough at the base of the press to collect the juice, and a car jack to provide the necessary pressure.

PREFERMENTATION ADDITIONS

Once you've squeezed your apples and filled your fermenting vessel (leaving an inch or so of headspace at the top), there are a couple of chemicals you may want to consider adding before fermentation. Using sulfite (in the form of a Campden tablet) will kill off the unwanted yeasts that can add dirty flavors to your cider, while also allowing more favorable yeasts to grow. However, you may wish to leave sulfite out, especially if you intend to serve your hard cider to anyone with a sulfite allergy.

If you've used predominantly culinary apples, it's also advisable to add some pectic enzyme at this point to prevent a pectin buildup in the cider, which can lead to haziness and unattractive, lava-lamp-style blobs in the finished drink.

ADDING/NOT ADDING YEAST

Wild yeasts grow naturally on (and in) the apples themselves, and they will begin to multiply in your juice. After a couple of days, fermentation should start in earnest. Although this natural process can produce exciting, complex flavors, fermenting with wild yeasts can be a bit unpredictable and, er, wild. You may wish to play it safe by using a store-bought cider yeast; when added to the juice, the cultured yeast will crowd out the wildlings and commence the fermentation process.

MAKER'S NOTES: HOW MANY APPLES?

To make a 1-gallon carboy of cider, you'll need to collect around 20 pounds of apples. Of course a lot depends on the varieties you have to hand (some apples are juicier than others) and what methods you are deploying to mill the apples and tease out the juice.

We've based the apple quantities in the following recipes on using the "fencepost and trug" method for milling, and a basket press for squeezing.

WHAT CAN GO WRONG?

If you notice something amiss, don't panic! Chances are there's an easy remedy.

Film yeast: This tends to appear before fermentation has started, and is caused by the ingress of air. Although it looks unpleasant, it should only affect the surface layer providing you catch it quickly enough. It's best to remove it with a slotted spoon and fit an airlock to prevent any nasty recurrences.

Stuck fermentation: Sometimes your cider may stop fermenting, despite the presence of fermentable sugar within. A vigorous stir with a long-handled spoon for 20 minutes should help get things going; failing that, try adding in some yeast nutrient and moving the fermenter to somewhere warmer.

Acetification: Exposing fermented cider to air, using unclean equipment and the dreaded vinegar fly all contribute to this sour, vinegary taint. To avoid it, ensure that all caps, bungs and airlocks are correctly fitted to your cider vessels, and only allow sterilized tools to come into contact with your precious juice.

Ropiness: A horrible affliction, turning cider into a thick, oily soup. It's caused by lactic-acid bacteria and occurs more commonly in cider that has not been sulfated. A lively stirring, followed by the addition of two Campden tablets per gallon, should remedy the problem.

KEEP IT TIGHT

During the initial stages of fermentation, when the yeast cells are busy multiplying, the juice will benefit from exposure to air. This will help the yeast grow strong cell walls, so plug the fermenter with a cotton ball to allow air in but prevent any airborne contamination. As the initial frothing subsides, replace the cotton ball plug with an airlock.

RACKING AND FINISHING

Your hard cider should continue to ferment for anything from two weeks to several months, depending on the type of apples and the ambient temperature where you are storing the fermenting vessels. If the cider is left in a cold shed or garage, fermentation will progress more slowly than if it is kept indoors, but when it comes to fermentation, slower is generally considered better, as the cider will tend to better retain its fruity flavors.

Before your hard cider is ready for bottling, it is worth siphoning it into a clean carboy, leaving behind the dirty deposits (a process known as "racking"). This should be done as the fermentation is close to finishing. When you are ready to bottle, check that the fermentation has finished by taking a gravity reading with a hydrometer. A figure of 1.005 or below indicates that it is ready. You may wish to delay racking for a month or so to see if a malolactic fermentation happens (see opposite).

Before bottling, add 1 Campden tablet per 1 gallon of cider for protection against bacterial infection.

CUSTOMIZING YOUR HARD CIDER

If you follow our instructions, you should end up with a nice, dry cider. It's a little more complicated for anything sweeter.

"Keeving" is a traditional way of retaining sweetness in hard cider, favored by the French and the most patient of cidermakers. It's a dark art, involving the encouragement of calcium to react with the pectin in a juice made from low-nutrient apples. The resulting naturally sweet cider can be bottled without risk of refermentation.

For the small-scale, amateur cidermaker, by far the easiest way of creating a sweeter hard cider is to add an artificial, nonfermentable sweetener at bottling stage. Sucralose is the ideal (if expensive) addition. For those who like fizzy, add ¼ ounce of sugar to every 4 cups before bottling. This will encourage a secondary fermentation and, although this will produce some sediment, it's a good trade-off for a bit of sparkle.

MALOLACTIC FERMENTATION

If you are lucky, this miraculous chemical process will occur when the weather warms up in spring and promotes autolysis in the bed of lees on which your cider sits. The welcome bacteria produced will lower the acidity in the cider and in turn produce a smoother, fuller flavor.

Making_time: 1 hour | **Fermenting time**: 2 to 6 months | **Maturing time**: 4 months

FARMHOUSE HARD CIDER

Some may say this is the greatest drink known to man; those who have had unfortunate experiences with it in their youth will tell you it's one of the worst. But put away your preconceptions . . . this will taste absolutely nothing like some of the bottled hard cider you get from the store. This is how to make a no-nonsense dry cider, pure and simple, just the way it should be.

20 pounds apples (all cider
   apples, or a mix of cooking
   and eating apples; see page 61)
1 Campden tablet

OPTIONAL
cider yeast
1 teaspoon pectic enzyme
1 teaspoon sugar per bottle,
   for priming

1. Prepare your apples for milling. Wash them if you've collected them from the orchard floor, and throw away any rotten ones.

2. Halve or quarter the apples, then mill them using one of the methods described on page 46.

3. Load the pulp into your press, or whatever you plan to use for pressing, then squeeze out the juice directly into a carboy.

4. Add 1 Campden tablet to the carboy, cover and leave for 24 hours.

5. Loosely plug the carboy with a cotton ball and wait patiently for fermentation to begin. It should start after a few days, but if you don't trust Mother Nature and her wild yeasts, add cider yeast to help her along. Adding some additional pectic enzyme at this stage will reduce the risk of hazy cider and pectin blobs.

6. After the initial fermentation has settled down, fit an airlock and put the carboy somewhere cool, and continue to ferment for several weeks.

7. Rack the young cider into a clean carboy when the bubbles passing through the airlock have slowed, and you have a good bed of lees.

8. Continue to ferment. When bubbles have ceased passing through the airlock, take a hydrometer reading. Anything below a gravity of 1.005 is ready to rack before bottling.

9. Add a teaspoon of sugar to each bottle to prime if you want a bit of fizz. This will also take the edge off the dryness.

RICH'S TIP
SWEET TOOTH?
Those not accustomed to the delights of a fully dry cider may need a bit of help. Try adding a teaspoon of artificial, nonfermentable sweetener such as sucralose before capping.

Making time: 1 hour | **Fermenting time**: 2 to 6 months | **Maturing time**: 2 to 4 months

CYSER

Long before the current trend of customizing hard cider with all manner of fruity additions, honey was regularly used to bring additional flavor to fermented apple juice and make a drink known as cyser. Unlike the lengthy wait for a more traditional mead, this golden-hued, nectar is made in the fall and will be ready in time for summer supping. Just be wary of the sting in the tail; cyser is somewhat alcoholic, and will leave your head feeling like a hive full of angry bees if you don't treat it with the respect it deserves.

18 cups Farmhouse Hard Cider
  (see opposite)
1⅛ pounds honey

1. Follow our easy instructions for Farmhouse Hard Cider on the opposite page, then return to this recipe after you rack the cider for the first time.

2. Take a jar of honey and heat it gently by immersing it in a pan of hot water. This will make it easier to pour.

3. Pour the honey into your carboy of cider and give it a good stir. The honey won't completely combine with the cider; it will tend to sit at the bottom of the carboy. This is not a problem. Do not fret.

4. Replace the airlock and stow your carboy somewhere safe. Fermentation will now recommence, with the sugars from the honey giving the yeast renewed vigor.

5. When the fermentation has stopped, or bubbles are passing very slowly through the airlock, rack off the cider into another clean vessel, refit the airlock and allow the cyser to ferment to a finish.

6. Your cyser should be ready for summer fun, but like all hard ciders, it will benefit from a few months' maturing.

 **Making time:** 1 hour | **Fermenting time:** 6 months | **Maturing time:** 4 months

PEAR & GINGER HARD CIDER

Hard cider purists, avert your eyes. Although the mixing of these flavors will probably get us into trouble with the traditionalists, we have our reasons . . . Unless you are lucky enough to get hold of perry pears, the more commonly found dessert varieties tend to be too soft to press and rather bland on their own. Using a combination of apples and pears* makes the juice easier to extract, and the nonfermentable sugars found in pears will give this drink a slight residual sweetness. We've added the ginger for bite . . . Grrrrr.

7¾ pounds apples
7¾ pounds pears
2-inch piece gingerroot, peeled
  and roughly chopped
1 Campden tablet

OPTIONAL
cider yeast
1 teaspoon pectic enzyme
1 teaspoon sugar per bottle,
  for priming

1. Prepare your fruit by washing it. Throw out any badly bruised specimens.

2. Quarter the fruit, then mill using one of the methods described on page 46.

3. Load the pulp into a press, squeeze and fill your carboy with the resulting juice, and throw in the chopped ginger.

4. Add 1 Campden tablet to the carboy, cover and leave in a cool place 24 hours.

5. Add the cider yeast and pectic enzyme (if using), and loosely bung the carboy with a cotton ball.

6. Fermentation should begin after a few days. When the initial fermentation has settled down, fit an airlock, put the carboy somewhere cool and leave to ferment for several weeks.

7. Rack the liquid into a clean carboy when the bubbles have slowed and you have a good bed of lees. You may wish to carry some sediment over when racking to encourage malolactic fermentation (see page 51).

8. Continue to ferment. When the bubbles have ceased passing through the airlock, take a hydrometer reading. Anything below a gravity of 1.005 is ready to rack before bottling.

9. Add 1 teaspoon of sugar to each bottle if you want a slight fizz when opening.

A NOTE ABOUT PERRY

Not to be confused with pear cider, a true "perry" is made solely from perry pears. Although quite rare, you'll know when you spot a perry pear tree . . . they are huge, and were often used as windbreaks in traditional cider orchards.

*In England, "apples and pears" is Cockney rhyming slang for "stairs." As in, "I have consumed too much pear cider and I am now finding it difficult to climb the apples and pears."

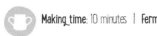 **Making time**: 10 minutes | **Fermenting/Infusing time**: 4 to 5 weeks

SLIDER

"Slider" is the name given to a hard cider that has been infused with the gin-soaked, boozy berries left over from the making of sloe gin (see page 118). The astringent sloes will bless the cider with their subtle almond flavors, while giving it a sneaky kick of gin for good measure. This drink can turn out quite alcoholic, and can catch out the unwary imbiber, so treat it as a slow-sipping summer drink or serve warm with added cloves and a pinch of cinnamon for a real winter warmer.

19 cups hard cider
2½ cups gin-infused
    sloes

1. Decant and bottle your sloe gin (see page 118), but leave the soggy, booze-infused sloes beind in the carboy.

2. Find a few bottles of Farmhouse Hard Cider (see page 52) that you are willing to give up . . . it's for a very good cause. Pour in enough cider to fill the carboy, and save* any surplus.

3. The gin-soaked sloes contain sugar, which will reawaken fermentation in the cider. Fit an airlock to the carboy to prevent an explosive gassy mess.

4. Leave the carboy in a cool place for 2 to 3 weeks for the sloes to infuse and release their boozy goodness, then decant the cider from the berries into another clean carboy and refit the airlock.

5. Wait another 2 weeks and, providing fermentation has ceased, you're ready to bottle.

6. You can leave this drink to mellow in the bottle for a few months if you like, but we drink ours soon after bottling to enjoy the full tarty taste.

BLACK(THORN) MAGIC
According to ancient folklore, burning an incense made from the wood, thorns and berries of the sloe bush will banish negativity and self-doubt. Your slider WILL taste fantastic.

ALTERNATIVELY . . .
Squeeze some vodka-infused damsons (see page 122) through the neck of your carboy to create a potent "damder." You could even try steeping the whiskey-blessed raspberries from page 120 to make a "rumpy" (raspberry scrumpy).

*And by "save," we mean "drink."

Making time: 1 hour | **Fermenting time**: 2 to 6 months | **Maturing time**: 4 months

BRAMBLE HARD CIDER

This dark and fruity summertime sipper pairs the blackberry—princely hedgerow foraging fodder—with our favorite fruit bar none (apples). It's a classy combination that will evoke memories of lazy, hazy summer afternoons. The blackberry flavors mellow through the fermentation process but will give the drink a distinctive, tangy finish and provide the dye for this hard cider's inky hue.

33 pounds apples (either cider apples or a mix of cookers and eaters; you can throw a few crab apples into the mix if you like)
4 cups blackberries
1 Campden tablet

OPTIONAL
cider yeast
pectic enzyme
1 teaspoon sugar per bottle, for priming

1. Scour the hedgerows for your bounty—blackberries are in plentiful supply as the fall arrives. Cider apples will produce a better drink, but a 50:50 mix of cooking and eating apples will work. Prepare your apples for milling. Wash them if they're from the orchard floor, and throw away any rotten ones.

2. Halve or quarter the apples, then mill them using one of the methods described on page 46. Load the pulp into your press, mixing in the blackberries as you go. Squeeze out the juice directly into a sterilized carboy.

3. Add 1 Campden tablet to the carboy, cover with a stopper and leave in a cool place for 24 hours.

4. Add pectic enzyme and yeast if using, loosely plug the carboy with a cotton ball and await fermentation, which should start any time from 2 days to 2 weeks.

5. After the initial fermentation has calmed sufficiently, fit an airlock, put the carboy somewhere cool and leave to ferment for several weeks.

6. When the fermentation has stopped, or bubbles are passing very slowly through the airlock, rack off the young cider from the lees into another clean vessel, and refit the airlock.

7. Continue to ferment. When the bubbles have ceased passing through the airlock, take a hydrometer reading (see page 11). Cider below a gravity of 1.005 is ready to rack before bottling.

8. Add 1 teaspoon of sugar to each bottle for a lightly sparkling booze. Your Bramble Hard Cider should be ready to drink by late spring/early summertime, but will improve with age, becoming less acidic if left to mature a few months longer.

DRINK FOR VICTORY

Blackberries are considered a "weed of national significance" and an "invasive species" by the Australian government. Aussies, forage this menace to extinction and drink yourself free from its prickly clasp!

Making time: 5 minutes | Infusing time: 2 to 3 days

SCRUMPLEFLOWER

A farmhouse hard cider made in the fall should be ready to sample around the time the hedgerows are bursting with blooms of elderflower. As with countless cidermakers before him, an overexuberant tasting session of appley nectar led Rich to inadvertently wander into those floral hedges and experience their intoxicating whiff up close. Such encounters could be the inspiration behind this recipe, an ingenious blend of flower and fruit that we call "scrumpleflower."

18 cups Farmhouse Hard Cider
  (see page 52)
5 large elderflower blooms,
  destalked

1. Follow our easy instructions for Farmhouse Hard Cider on page 52, then flip back to this page after you rack the cider for the first time. (You can, of course, buy some hard cider to make your scrumpleflower with, but we would consider this cheating.)

2. Grab 5 hand-sized* blooms of elderflower from your nearest elderflower bush. Shake them to remove any nasty bugs, then wash them just to be sure.

3. Remove the flowers from the green stalks with a fork, then put the stalks in the trash and the flowers in a muslin bag or similar.

4. Push the muslin bag through the neck of your cider-bearing carboy, then replace the bung. Put the carboy in a safe place, and wait 2 to 3 days for the flowers to infuse.

5. Remove the bag before racking into a clean carboy, and then bottling.

RICH'S TIP
Only willing to spare a bottle of cider? Pour 2 cups into a sealable jar, add a bloom of fresh, destalked flowers and wait 3 to 4 hours before filtering and imbibing.

Make it 6 if you have particularly small hands.

🍎 APPLES

As obsessive cidermakers, it's no surprise that we would claim the apple as the world's greatest fruit. There's more to apples than just their magical, fermented juice-bringing properties though; the complex and varied mix of sugars and acids contained within make them the perfect fruit for a multitude of home-brewing projects—whether steeping, brewing, chopping or squeezing.

There are four main categories of apple, all of which can be utilized by the shrewd home brewer.

COOKING AND EATING APPLES
Great for wine making, even better for hard cider making, a blend of cooking and eating apples will give you a sharp, clean-tasting hard cider. Culinary apples are ideal for infusing with strong spirits, and are great for bringing acidity to fruity wine blends.

CIDER APPLES
These are by far our favorite type of apple, but are not that widespread outside of traditional hard cider-making regions. They have characteristically high sugar levels and astringency and are categorized into four groups: sweet, sharp, bittersweet and bitter-sharp, depending on the sugar, acid and tannin balance. For hard cider-making purposes a predominance of bittersweet apples mixed with some dessert/culinary varieties should give you prize-winning results.

SEEDLING APPLES
"Seedling" is the term used for trees that have grown from seed. You'll find plenty of these at the sides of roads and railway lines, germinated from apples cast aside by hungry travelers. The resulting apples can vary in quality, so give them a taste before gathering to avoid disappointment.

CRAB APPLES
Often too sour and astringent for eating, crab apples are great for adding depth to insipid juice destined for hard cider making. They also make a mean wine (see page 24) but again, try before fermenting.

GROW YOUR OWN CIDER ORCHARD

An orchard is classified as a collection of four or more fruit trees. Got the space . . . then what are you waiting for?

1. Select your trees: Your trees will require comparable pollinators, so check before buying. For an excellent mix from the same pollination group, try Yarlington Mill, Sweet Coppin, Black Dabinett and Fair Maid of Devon.

2. Choose your rootstock: A "half-standard" tree will grow to around 13 feet, while a shorter "bush" will be more suitable for smaller yards.

3. Time it right: Plant out between late fall and early spring in a sunny, sheltered site that has moderately fertile, well-drained soil. Don't add compost to the planting site as this will lead to weak, lazy roots.

4. Dig for victory: For each tree, dig a hole no deeper than the root system, but three times as wide.

5. Aftercare: Mulch around the base to keep weeds at bay, then water thoroughly. Water again the day after planting, then once a week during the summer months. Your apple trees should bear fruit after 3 years.

 **Making time**: 1 hour 20 minutes

ROSEHIP HARD CIDER

Flavored hard ciders are very popular, and one of the easiest ways of pimping your appley booze is with a simple syrup. Rich has dropped many nectars into his hard ciders, but his favorite comes courtesy of the rosehip—its sweet, tangy flavors can elevate even the driest cider to new heights.

FOR THE ROSEHIP SYRUP
2½ cups rosehips,
    roughly chopped
scant 1¼ cups sugar

TO SERVE (PER GLASS)
2½ cups dry hard cider
2 tablespoons rosehip syrup

1. First, grab a bottle of your homemade Farmhouse Hard Cider (see page 52), or hot-foot it to your local booze emporium and choose a nice, dry variety.

2. To make the rosehip syrup, mash up your hips using a mortar and pestle or something similar, then put in a saucepan with a scant 2½ cups water.

3. Bring to a boil, then simmer for 15 minutes.

4. Remove from heat, then strain through a muslin cloth into a saucepan, leaving the pulp to sit and drain for around 30 minutes.

5. Strain again through a clean muslin cloth. This is to ensure that no irritating rosehip hairs make their way into the final syrup.

6. Add to a pan with the sugar, then heat slowly, stirring until the sugar is dissolved.

7. Continue to boil for 3 to 5 minutes, skimming off any scum that rises with a wooden spoon.

8. Pour into sterilized bottles when cool, and store in a refrigerator. Once opened, your syrup should last 2 weeks—but unopened bottles will last a year or so.

9. Chill your cider in the refrigerator, then add the syrup to the cider, giving the drink a gentle stir.

MAKER'S NOTES:
VARIATIONS

Inspired by our original rosehip hard cider? Then get syrupy with these tasty alternatives:

› Blackberries, elderberries, strawberries and raspberries all work wonders.

› Use blackcurrants for a delicious "cider and black."

SERVING SUGGESTION

Your rosehip syrup can also be used in other wondrous ways: dilute with water for a refreshing cordial, liven up a plain fizzy wine or drizzle over pancakes, ice cream or yogurt for a fruity treat.

VITAMIN DEFICIENCY

Rosehips are loaded with vitamin C, and were collected during the Second World War as a replacement for difficult-to-obtain citrus fruits. Sadly, boiling them removes most of the health-giving minerals, so you can't really claim this drink as contributing to your daily fruit intake.

Making time: 5 minutes | **Infusing time**: 4 to 5 days

HOPPED HARD CIDER

When two worlds collide: this traditionalist-enraging hard cider curio reaches over to the craft beer community and gives it a big old whiskery hug. The addition of hops will impart thrilling flavors to a fully fermented hard cider, but because no boiling is involved, they will not add bitterness. It's an exciting IPA/cider mash-up for those who seek something hip and hoppy.

18 cups hard cider
¼ ounce hops

1. Take a fully fermented, 1.1-gallon carboy of your finest hard cider. Don't be tempted to use a bad batch and hope the hops mask the nasty taste. We've tried it. It doesn't work...

2. Select your hops—the beauty of this recipe is its customizability, but as a guide, hops that are used for the brewing of IPAs work just fine. To start, we would suggest adding approximately ¼ ounce of a citrussy hop such as Cascade, then experiment from there.

3. Sprinkle the hops into the carboy of cider, then refit the airlock to keep the air and other nasties out. You may wish to add your hops to the cider in a muslin bag for ease of filtering when it comes to bottling.

4. Leave the carboy in a cool place for 4 to 5 days. The longer you leave it, the hoppier your final cider will taste.

5. Filter your hoppy cider though a muslin cloth into sterilized bottles. Just don't offer to share it with a cider traditionalist!

BREWER'S NOTES: VARIATIONS

You can test out different hop combinations by adding small quantities to a glass of hard cider and taking copious notes. Here's a guide to the flavors you can expect.

Citrussy hops:
› Cascade
› Citra
› Simcoe Centennial
› First Gold

Spicy hops:
› Saaz
› Willamette
› Golding
› Nugget
› Chinook

Making_time: 25 minutes

RICH'S HOT TODDY

Need an extra-strong, soothing tipple to chase away the winter blues? Then try this for size . . . our bubbling brew will take the chill off the frostiest of nights and bring color to the palest of cheeks. It also has remarkable healing properties for those suffering from coughs and sneezes; the heady combination of alcohol, honey and spices will soothe and anesthetize in equal measures. Indeed, it will either knock the cold out of you or knock you out cold.

2 cups dry hard cider
2 teaspoons lemon juice
3 tablespoons brandy
4 cloves
1 cinnamon stick
1-inch piece gingerroot,
  peeled and grated
2 tablespoons honey

1. Put the cider, juice, brandy and spices into a saucepan and warm gently over low heat. Don't let the liquid boil, as this will burn off the alcohol, which is the sort of thing we like to discourage.

2. After a couple of minutes add the honey, and stir until dissolved.

3. Continue heating for about 10 minutes, giving it a cursory stir now and again. Savor its heavenly scent!

4. Pour through a strainer into heat-resistant glasses or mugs, inhale the soothing aromas—then enjoy.

ALTERNATIVELY . . .

No heat? No problem! The ingredients from this recipe can be easily adapted to make a delicious cidery cocktail.

Pour a scant 1¼ cups hard cider, 3 tablespoons brandy, 2 teaspoons lemon juice, 1 tablespoon honey and a 1-inch piece grated gingerroot into a measuring pitcher along with a handful of ice cubes, and stir to combine. Strain into two serving glasses and garnish with a slice of orange. Easy!

 **Making_time:** 1 hour

LAMBSWOOL

Traditionally drunk in England on Twelfth Night, this unusually named pagan throwback is consumed during the practice of "wassailing," the ancient ritual of awakening apple trees from their winter slumber to encourage a bountiful apple crop in the coming year. Custom dictates that wassailers drink from a communal cup of lambswool while singing the wassail song (see below). Pots and pans are beaten with sticks to drive away any harvest-spoiling entities and, in some of the more rowdy ceremonies, shotguns* are fired into the branches of the quivering apple trees. Planning to hold your own backyard wassail? Appease frightened neighbors by offering them a cup of this steamy beverage . . .

6 medium apples
30 cloves
1½ cups demerara sugar
6 cups dry hard cider
a few pinches of ground nutmeg
1-inch piece gingerroot, peeled
    and grated

1. Core the apples and press 5 cloves into the skin of each. Pour 1 tablespoon of demerara sugar into each apple, then cook on a baking sheet in the oven at 350°F for 30 to 35 minutes. Check regularly to avoid the apples burning.

2. Meanwhile, warm your cider gently in a pan, adding the remaining sugar, the nutmeg and grated ginger.

3. Stir gently until the sugar is dissolved, then continue to heat gently for 15 to 20 minutes, stirring occasionally.

4. Remove the baked apples from the oven and mash them in a bowl with a potato masher or similar. (Let the apples cool before mashing . . . hot pulp spilled onto skin will make you yelp.) Remove the apple skin with a fork first if you want aesthetically pleasing lambswool.

5. Add the mashed apples to the pan, and use a whisk to combine them with the cider and spices. The more you whisk it, the more it is said to resemble lambswool, hence the name. (Albeit a filthy lamb that's been rolling around in an orchard.)

6. Ladle the finished drink into a communal bowl, adding a further sprinkle of nutmeg before passing cups around to eager wassailers.

THE WASSAIL SONG

Here stands a good apple tree, stand fast root!

Every little twig bear an apple big.

Hats full, caps full, and three score sacks full,

Hip hip hurrah!

*We'd question the logic of mixing firearms with hard cider-based beverages, but there's no accounting for some old English traditions!

GOOD SPIRITS

This hot apple booze should be served with toast, some of which is then dipped into the lambswool and hung on the branches of apple trees as an offering to the tree spirits. Lambswool is also poured under the tree to coax the roots into healthy growth. In certain cases, bad lambswool is poured under the tree to get rid of it quickly.

BEER, ALE & LAGER BASICS

If you've never attempted to brew beer then you could be forgiven for thinking that you need to learn a new language and a science before you even begin. At first sight, beer recipes—with their precise timings, temperatures and terminology—can be off-putting to the uninitiated. But while these instructions are important for the professionals and legions of ultra-eager homebrew fans, for us kitchen brewers who simply want a good pint, things are much, much simpler.

There are three basic ways of getting hold of the necessary grain-based ingredients required to make beer. The simplest is to use a kit—all the contents are ready prepared and you simply follow the instructions on the pack to brew up the designated beer style. At the other end of the scale is "full grain" brewing, where you start with roasted grains and extract their goodness yourself so that they're ready to be turned into beer. We use an in-between method known as "extract brewing." Here you'll have access to a vast range of ingredients, but the hard work of processing has already been done, making brewing much easier, while still allowing for infinite possibilities to craft your own delicious beers.

To make things easier still, we start small. Kits and beginner recipes tend to be developed for 5-gallon brews, which, although small in comparison to commercial brewery quantities, demand fairly big pieces of kit in order to make a full batch. And although 5 gallons seems like a good volume for your efforts, it leaves you with quite a lot of beer to consume before you're ready to try out your next recipe (and it seems even more if a batch goes wrong). So we advocate using 1-gallon brews. You can manage these in the smallest of kitchens, you won't need to buy large pieces of equipment and you can experiment with new styles and flavors without it costing a fortune each time. You'll be rewarded with around seven 17-fluid ounce bottles of beer per recipe (or use smaller bottles to spread the wealth), but the process is so quick and easy that when the bug strikes you'll find yourself brewing every week. Once you discover a recipe you like it's easy to double it or progress to a larger brew. We often brew two beers simultaneously, tweaking the ingredients for each beer to unearth exciting new flavors.

ESSENTIAL EQUIPMENT

> Fermentation vessel
> Large pot with lid for boiling
> Stirring spoon
> Grain bag, muslin cloth or
> fine sieve for straining
> Thermometer
> Hydrometer and narrow
> measuring cylinder
> Siphoning tube
> Bottles (and crown capper
> if using crown caps)

NICK'S TIP
WATER

For most of the lighter beers and lagers, soft water is preferable to hard water. If your water is especially hard, it can be softened by adding gypsum salts (seek advice on how to treat your own water). Alternatively, bulk-buy cheap bottled water from the grocery store.

HOW IS BEER MADE?

As with wine, beer is created by fermentation—using yeast to convert sugar into alcohol. For most beers, the sugar comes from barley, but only once it has been "malted." This technique allows the grains to germinate, which converts their starches into sugars, before the process is halted through roasting in a kiln. The grains are then milled to allow their sugars to be extracted by soaking in water at precise temperatures and times, known as "mashing." Our recipes use ready mashed and processed "malt extracts" which come in liquid (LME) or dried (DME) forms. We'll also occasionally throw in a few specialty grains that will give you a basic experience of the mashing process.

WHAT GIVES EACH BEER ITS UNIQUE CHARACTERISTICS?

The huge variety of beer styles available is a result of the near-infinite possible combinations of different types of malted barley with alternative grains, hops and other flavored ingredients. For example, using barley that has been roasted for longer and at a higher temperature will give beer a darker color and toastier flavors. Different varieties of hops will change the bitter characteristics and aromas of the finished product. And even the type of yeast used can develop flavors in different and exciting ways.

PREPARING FOR FERMENTING

In order to prepare your ingredients for fermenting you'll first need to boil the extract with water, adding hops and other flavors at various stages of the process. When complete this liquid should be given a good stir to oxygenate it, and cooled as quickly as possible—we do this by only using half the water for a boil and keeping the remainder in the refrigerator. Putting your boiling pot in a sink of iced water also helps.

Once the liquid has cooled (to below 75°F) you're ready to add the yeast and allow it to get to work on those sugars. Yeast is supplied in various liquid or dry forms, the use of which varies according to type and manufacturer. For the beginner we recommend individual sachets, which you should add according to the instructions on the packet. For most beers in this book a warm (but not hot) room at around 60 to 75°F is sufficient for fermentation, although lagers prefer it cooler.

WHAT FERMENTATION VESSEL TO USE

For our 1-gallon batches we use either food-grade buckets, fitted with a lid but leaving a small gap to allow gas to escape, or a glass carboy and airlock. They both have their pros and cons, as outlined below.

Buckets:
› Light and easy to carry
› Large opening makes it easy to deposit ingredients into the bucket (but also easier for unwanted items to fall in)
› Plenty of space for fermentation, and easy to increase beer quantity
› Opaque plastic makes it harder to see the layer of sediment, making siphoning into bottles trickier
› Plastic will degrade and get scratched over time and will eventually need replacing

Carboys:
› Providing you don't break them, they'll last forever
› You can see the contents easily, making siphoning a simple task
› The airlock is a secure device that won't allow outside elements to infiltrate and will also enable you to monitor fermentation more easily
› If you fill it up too much a vigorous fermentation will burst through the airlock, making a mess (if this happens, simply replace the airlock with a clean one)
› Relatively heavy to carry around and hard to clean

BREWING TERMS

Adjuncts:
Additional ingredients added to a basic recipe.

Hopping:
Adding hops during various stages of a boil.

Hot break:
Rapidly rising foam when the wort boils.

Krausen:
The frothy crust that forms on the beer during fermentation.

Mash:
Steeping grains in water to extract sugar and flavor.

Priming:
Adding sugar at bottling stage to help condition the beer and give it some fizz.

Wort:
The malty liquid that is brought to a boil.

BREWER'S NOTES: CLEAR BEER

We don't use clarifying agents in our recipes—a slight haziness has never concerned us. If you prefer crystal-clear beer, the most popular solution for home brewers is to add the red algae "Irish moss" to a boil.

BOTTLING

Most of our beers will have finished fermenting after 1 to 2 weeks, but there's no harm in leaving a beer that has fermented early for the full 2 weeks—the conditioning might even improve it. To be certain fermentation has ceased you'll need to take a hydrometer reading. Siphon off a small amount of beer into a narrow tube and dip the hydrometer into it. If the reading is a gravity of 1.012 or lower, it should be ready. However, check again the next day to make sure it's the same level and therefore stable. And don't return the siphoned-off drink to the main batch in case it introduces infection—drink it instead!

You're then ready to siphon the liquid into beer bottles. Your first few attempts could get messy, with minor spillages highly likely, and it's a much easier task with two people. However, you'll soon become adept at the process. Choose good, sturdy glass beer bottles (you can recycle your own), either complete with swing tops or ones that can be fitted with crown caps. Homebrew beers benefit from a bit of bottle conditioning and fizz when opened; a small amount of fermentation within the bottles can be created by adding half a teaspoon of sugar to each bottle before the beer goes in.

Stand your sterilized bottles on a towel or put them in a bucket (to avoid beer on the kitchen floor) at a lower level than the beer you're about to siphon. Stick one end of a sterilized tube into the beer (just above the sediment) and gently suck the other end until you get the taste of beer in your mouth. Direct the flowing beer into the bottles and fill them until you approach the layer of sediment. If you suck out a little dirt, don't despair, as it'll settle to the bottom of the bottle, giving you another chance to avoid it when pouring the beer into a glass.

Fit the bottle lid and return it to your warm location for a day to allow the sugar to ferment. Beer is then best stored in a cool place. With most beers you can happily drink your hard work within 1 week of bottling, but many of our recipes will benefit from maturing for longer.

HOW STRONG IS MY BEER?

Most recipes in this book will produce beer ranging from 4% to 5.5% alcohol by volume (ABV), but there are too many random factors to give exact percentages for each beer. To find out the strength of your brews you'll need to take a hydrometer reading before adding yeast, and another before bottling. There are numerous online calculators that use these figures to determine your beer's ABV percentage, but as a guide we've given you three examples:

› Original gravity—1.040; final gravity—1.010; alcohol—3.94%

› Original gravity—1.045; final gravity—1.010; alcohol—4.59%

› Original gravity—1.050; final gravity—1.010; alcohol—5.25%

STERILIZE!
As with all fermented drinks, make sure you sterilize every piece of equipment used at all stages of the process.

Making time: 2 hours | **Fermenting time**: 1 to 2 weeks | **Maturing time**: 1 week

BASIC BEER

For a good, cheap and easy beer you can't go far wrong with this recipe. Most serious brewers will scoff at the use of sugar, especially in such high quantities, but its use has advantages for the newcomer. Besides bringing your beer to a decent strength while keeping costs down, it will also give your palate the experience of tasting a beer in its simplest form—and the end result is still a hugely enjoyable drink. From this recipe you can start to explore more complex brews by replacing the sugar with some of the various styles of dry malt extract, or by trying different hops to see how they alter the flavor and characteristics of your beer.

1¼ cups liquid malt extract
  (light or amber)
1 small handful of bittering hops
1 cup white sugar
ale or brewer's yeast
½ teaspoon white sugar per
  bottle, for priming

1. Sterilize all the equipment. Boil 9 cups water, pour into a sealed container and let cool in the refrigerator.

2. Heat 9 cups water in a large pan and add the malt extract, stirring until it has dissolved.

3. Bring to a boil until the liquid rapidly foams. Turn down the heat to prevent it boiling over, then turn the heat back up and repeat the process until the rapid foaming ceases.

4. Add the hops and sugar, partially cover the pan and keep it at a gentle boil for 45 minutes. Combine this liquid with the water from the refrigerator, give it a vigorous stir and let cool.

5. Strain the liquid into your fermentation vessel of choice and pitch the yeast, following the instructions on the packet. If using a carboy, fit an airlock, and for a bucket, cover with a lid (leaving a slight gap for gas to escape). Put it somewhere warm—around 60 to 75°F is ideal.

6. When fermentation has finished, usually after 1 to 2 weeks, you're ready to bottle your brew. Sterilize the bottles and drop half a teaspoon of white sugar into each one. Carefully fill with beer using a siphon, stopping before you reach the sludge at the bottom of the fermenter.

7. Cap the bottles and gently shake to dissolve the sugar. Put them somewhere warm for a couple of days to kick-start the conditioning fermentation, then move to a cooler spot and allow at least 1 week for the beer to mature in the bottles before drinking.

NICK'S TIP
Conveniently, the amount of fermentable sugar in dry malt extract is almost the same as in pure white sugar. So if you vehemently object to the notion of brewing with sugar, or have practiced enough with the cheaper ingredient, then simply upgrade by replacing the white stuff with a dry malt extract of your choice.

Making time: 2 hours | **Fermenting time:** 1 to 2 weeks | **Maturing time:** 2 weeks

LONDON PORTER

If beer fan Nick were placed under intense pressure and forced to name his favorite beer, he might just splutter the word "porter." It's a black drink, getting its deep color and toasty flavors from the addition of heavily roasted malts. The style originated in 18th-century London, where it became a hit among the porting profession, hence its name, and was for a while the most popular style of beer in England. This recipe includes flaked barley, which, although not essential, gives the finished brew a boost to the body and a smooth creaminess to the head.

2¼ cups liquid malt extract
(light or amber)
⅖ cup black grain malt
⅖ cup flaked barley
1 handful of hops—bittering hops,
e.g. Admiral, Goldings or Target
suit the style
ale or brewer's yeast
½ teaspoon white sugar per
bottle, for priming

1. Heat 9 cups water in a large pan. When it approaches boiling point add the malt extract, black grain malt and flaked barley. The solid items can go in a grain bag if you have one.

2. Bring to a boil until the liquid rapidly foams. Turn down the heat to prevent it boiling over, then return it to a gentle boil.

3. After 15 minutes add the hops. Continue to heat at a steady boil a further 30 minutes. Keep a lid on the pan, but give the liquid an occasional stir.

4. Remove from the heat and mix with 9 cups preboiled and cooled water, to help bring the overall temperature down. Give it a good stir to aerate it, and when it has sufficiently cooled to below 75°F strain the liquid into your fermentation vessel of choice.

5. Add the yeast according to the instructions on the packet, and leave to ferment somewhere warm—around 60 to 75°F is ideal.

6. Fermentation should be finished after 1 to 2 weeks. Check by measuring the gravity with a hydrometer; if it reads 1.012 or below for a few consecutive days you're ready for bottling.

7. Prime the sterilized bottles with sugar as described in the basic beer recipe (see page 74) before filling them with beer. Put the bottles somewhere warm for 2 days to kick-start the conditioning fermentation, then move to a cooler location. Porters benefit from a minimum of 2 weeks maturing in the bottles.

NICK'S TIP
A THRILLER IN VANILLA
Strange as it sounds, the rich roasted-malt flavors of porter work with the unique aroma and spicy notes of vanilla. Try dropping a whole vanilla pod into your fermenting bucket with the beer.

INDIA PALE ALE

India Pale Ale (IPA) was born out of necessity in 19th-century England. By ramping up the alcohol content and using extra hops for their preservative powers, brewers were able to supply beers that were more likely to make the long ocean journey to India without spoiling. Until recently IPAs had drifted from their original hoppy heights to become nondescript, bland bitters. But American beer revivalists latched on to the style and used it as a base to play with new, intense hoppy flavors. Now the choice of IPAs is huge, which suits Rich, who makes a beeline for every new variant he finds—but even he thinks this recipe is one well worth coming back to.

¾ cup crushed crystal malt

4⅓ cups extra light dry malt extract

1 handful of bittering hops—e.g. Goldings, Target, Columbus

1 handful of aroma hops—e.g. Cascade, Nelson Sauvin, Citra

ale or brewer's yeast

½ teaspoon white sugar per bottle, for priming

1. Put the crushed crystal malt into a pan with 9 cups water (use a grain bag if you have one). Heat until the mixture reaches 150 to 160°F, then cover with a lid and steep 15 minutes at this temperature, stirring occasionally.

2. Remove the grains and add the malt extract. Bring to a boil until the liquid rapidly foams, then turn the heat down to keep it from boiling over.

3. Add the bittering hops and continue with a steady boil around 45 minutes. 15 minutes before the end of a boil, add half of the aroma hops to the pan.

4. When the 45 minutes are up, add the remaining aroma hops and remove from the heat. This will preserve the intense, fresh hop fragrance and add a level of complexity to the ale.

5. Add 9 cups preboiled and cooled water, to help bring the overall temperature down. Give it a good stir to aerate it, and when it has sufficiently cooled to below 75°F strain the liquid into your fermentation vessel of choice.

6. Add the yeast according to the instructions on the packet and leave to ferment somewhere warm—around 60 to 75°F is ideal.

7. Set aside in a warm place, and when fermentation has finished prime the sterilized bottles with sugar as described in the basic beer recipe (see page 74) before filling them with beer. Return the beer to a warm location for 2 days, then leave in a cool place at least 1 week to mature.

RICH'S TIP
HOPPING AROUND
Try playing around with different combinations of hops added at various stages of the boiling process to create truly unique IPAs.

WHEAT BEER

Visit a good German bar and you're almost guaranteed to see a wide choice of wheat beers. But, with the exception of Belgium, it'll be much harder to track one down in the rest of the world. Wheat beer has a long, proud history in Germany, with each region producing its own variation. This recipe is akin to a southern-style *Hefeweizen*, which can easily be given a Belgian makeover by the addition of orange peel and coriander seeds. The use of proper wheat beer yeast is important, as this helps bring out the beer's distinctive flavors (commonly described as "banana and cloves"), allowing the hops to take a backseat role. Wheat beers actually use a mixture of wheat and barley as their base grain, which, thankfully, should already be combined in your wheat malt extract.

1 cup flaked wheat
4 cups dry wheat malt extract
a few pinches of hops—
  Hallertauer, Saaz or Tettnanger
  are commonly used
wheat beer yeast
½ teaspoon sugar per bottle,
  for priming

1. Put the flaked wheat in a grain bag and steep in a pan containing 9 cups water by heating to a temperature of around 160°F, hold it there 20 minutes, stirring occasionally.

2. Remove the grain bag from the now-cloudy water, and stir in the dry wheat malt extract.

3. Bring to a boil until the liquid rapidly foams. Turn down the heat to prevent it boiling over, then return it to a gentle boil. Add the hops and maintain a steady boil 1 hour.

4. Remove from the heat and mix with 9 cups preboiled and cooled water, to help bring the overall temperature down. Give it a good stir to aerate it, and when it has sufficiently cooled to below 75°F strain the liquid into your fermentation vessel of choice.

BREWER'S NOTES: WITBIER

To make your wheat beer more akin to a Belgian *witbier*, add half a teaspoon of lightly cracked coriander seeds and the zest of ¼ orange for the last 20 minutes of a boil.

FLAKED WHEAT

Flaked wheat accentuates the sharp, wheaty flavor, aids smoothness and head retention, and gives the finished beer its distinctive hazy appearance. You can also use it in your breakfast granola.

5. Add the yeast according to the instructions on the packet and leave to ferment—the ideal temperature for wheat beer is 65 to 68°F, and it will take 1 to 2 weeks.

6. Prime the bottles with sugar (see page 74) before filling them. Allow at least 1 week for the beer to mature before drinking.

SERVING SUGGESTION

German wheat beer is traditionally served in a tall, narrow glass with a bulge at the top. Debate rages as to whether adding a slice of lemon is a good thing or not.

 HOPS

It may be the grains that do most of the hard work in the beer brewing process, but it's often the hops that take the glory. Hops give beer its unique bitter taste and aroma, and it's the brewer's job to select their preferred varieties for each style—adding them at just the right moment to take advantage of each hop's individual characteristics.

WHAT IS A HOP?

The hop is a climbing vine which grows as separate male and female plants, with the latter producing the conical green flowers that are used in brewing. These flowers are harvested in the fall when their oils are at their most aromatic, and are delivered to home brewers in a number of forms, most commonly freshly vacuum packed or pressed into pellets. Growing your own hops is relatively easy—simply plant the rhizomes before they begin their spring growth, and give them something tall to ramble over. They're also a fairly common sight growing wild in hedgerows.

USING HOPS

There are many varieties of hop, with each being rated according to its "alpha acid" content, which gives an indication of its bitterness. Hops with a high alpha acid rating tend to be added early in the boiling process to lend bitterness to the beer, while hops with a lower rating are often used at the end of a boil as a way of providing aroma and more subtle flavors. Complex brews will have combinations of hops added throughout the boiling process, building up unique flavors and aromas that show off the brewer's craft. We've kept things simple with our recipes, but once you get more familiar with their potential you can easily experiment, creating whole new beers just by changing what hops you use and how you use them.

TOP HOPS!
OUR FIVE FAVORITE HOP VARIETIES

Goldings: This workhorse hop can be used for many beer styles and is often used to provide both flavor and aroma. It never lets us down, making it our default hop for most recipes.

Hallertauer: A delicately spicy and lightly bitter German hop that complements the crispness of lager-style booze.

Cascade: This is a strong, aromatic hop, often described as having "grapefruit notes." Very popular in hop-packed, modern American ales.

Target: A classic British bitter hop for beefing up your brews. Packed with flavor, it's also not shy of releasing its hoppy aroma.

Nelson Sauvin: New Zealand is a hotbed of hop-growing activity, and this is one of its most popular new varieties. Fruity, fragrant and flavorsome.

Making time: 2 hours | **Fermenting time**: 4 to 6 weeks | **Maturing time**: 1 month

LAGER

It would be foolish of us to leave out the world's most popular beer style from this book, but it does mean presenting a recipe that requires a bit more precision brewing than most. You can blame it on the yeast. Unlike the rest of our beers, which use top-fermenting yeasts, lager's yeast is bottom fermenting—which requires lower temperatures, a few extra processes and a longer maturation time. But if you've got the patience and can give it the necessary cold environment,* a crisp and clean home-brewed lager is well worth the effort.

3⅛ cups extra light dry malt extract

½ cup dark cane sugar syrup

1 small handful of hops— Hallertauer, Saaz or Tettnanger are commonly used

lager yeast

½ teaspoon sugar per bottle, for priming

1. Heat 9 cups water in a large pan, and add the dry malt extract and dark cane sugar syrup. Stir until it has dissolved.

2. Bring to a boil until the liquid rapidly foams. Turn down the heat to prevent it boiling over, then return to a gentle boil. Add two-thirds of the hops and maintain a steady boil 45 minutes. The remaining hops go into the liquid for the last 5 minutes.

3. Remove from the heat and mix with 9 cups preboiled and cooled water, to help bring the overall temperature down. Give it a good stir to aerate it.

4. When the liquid has cooled, strain it into a fermenter. It's important to check the instructions on the yeast packet to make sure that it is pitched correctly and at the right temperature. The ideal temperature for fermentation is 45 to 55°F.

5. After 2 to 3 weeks, when fermentation has all but ceased (no more bubbles in an airlock, or a consistently low gravity reading of around 1.012 on successive days), you need to move it to somewhere warm (60 to 70°F) for 2 days. This reactivates fermentation in a process known as a "diacetyl rest," and will remove a few unwanted flavors.

6. After resting, rack the lager to a secondary fermenter and return it to the cool location, or somewhere colder if you can. Allow it to mature 2 to 3 weeks—a process known as "lagering."

**BREWER'S NOTES:
THE BIG SOFTIE**

Fussy lager demands soft water. If your tap turns out the hard stuff, we find that large, cheap bottles of water do the trick.

7. Follow standard bottling practices by priming with sugar (see the basic beer recipe on page 74) and leave it somewhere cool at least 1 month before opening.

We use Nick's cold and drafty attic during the winter months.

Making time: 2 hours | **Fermenting time**: 1 to 2 weeks | **Maturing time**: 2 weeks

HONEY ALE

Craft brewers often look at combining sugary ingredients with grains to alter the characteristics of their beers, but few of these ingredients are as rewarding as honey. It can add a lightness to any beer style, bringing with it a delicate taste of honey and subtle floral aromas. This beer is simple to make, but the resulting drink will get you buzzing—and if you're as impressed with it as we are, see what adding honey can do to other beer styles.

¾ cup crushed crystal malt

1¼ cups liquid malt extract (light or amber)

1 small handful of hops—made up of two-thirds bittering hops, and one-third aroma hops

generous ½ cup pasteurized honey

ale or brewer's yeast

½ teaspoon white sugar per bottle, for priming

MAKER'S NOTES: FIVE SUGARY SUPPLEMENTS

› Dark cane sugar syrup or corn syrup: Boosts alcohol strength without having a big impact on flavor.

› Molasses: Just a touch will give your beer a rich, toffee flavor—but try not to overdo it.

› Belgian candy sugar: Popular in Belgium for super-strong beers.

› Lactose (milk sugar): This sugar won't ferment out, so it's used to provide sweetness. Gives "milk stout" half of its name.

› Maple syrup: Lightens the beer in a similar way to honey. Beer and pancakes, anyone?

1. Put the crushed crystal malt into a pan with 9 cups water (use a grain bag if you have one)—honey's sweetness disappears during fermentation so the crystal malt will provide a sweet caramel kiss. Heat the water until it reaches 150 to 160°F, then cover and steep 15 minutes, maintaining this temperature and stirring occasionally.

2. Remove the grains and add the malt extract. Bring to a boil until the liquid rapidly foams, then turn the heat down to prevent it boiling over.

3. Add around two-thirds of the hops (ideally these should be bittering hops—see page 81) and continue with a steady boil around 45 minutes.

4. For the last 5 minutes of the boil add the honey and remaining hops (ideally aroma hops this time, see page 81).

5. Remove from the heat and mix with 9 cups preboiled and cooled water, to help bring the overall temperature down. Give it a good stir to aerate it, and when it has sufficiently cooled to below 75°F, strain the liquid into your fermentation vessel of choice.

6. Add the yeast according to the instructions on the packet and leave to ferment somewhere warm—around 60 to 75°F is ideal.

7. When fermentation has finished, prime the bottles with sugar as outlined in the basic beer recipe (see page 74). Put the beer somewhere warm 2 days, then leave in a cool place at least 2 weeks to mature before drinking.

PRESIDENTIAL ALES

In 2012, President Obama got the craft brewing scene excited when he released recipes for a White House Honey Ale and White House Honey Porter. The president's honey came from hives on the White House lawn.

Making time: 2¼ hours | **Fermenting time**: 1 to 2 weeks | **Maturing time**: 3 weeks

NICK'S LIQUORICE STOUT

We like dark beers. Our English Brown Ale (see page 92) is the epitome of a dark brown beery brew; our London Porter (see page 76) moves into even darker territory; but there is none more black than this beer, Nick's Liquorice Stout. It's a robust blend of black malts and roasted barley, is hopped to the max and has an extra black swirl of liquorice root. Not only is it our darkest beer, it's also the strongest beer in the book and should therefore be matured for longer and handled with the respect it deserves.

⅓ cup black malt
⅓ cup roasted barley
2½ cups liquid malt extract
   (light or amber)
1 stick of liquorice root
1 handful of bittering hops—e.g.
   Goldings, Target, Columbus
1 handful of aroma hops—e.g.
   Cascade, Nelson Sauvin, Citra
ale or brewer's yeast
½ teaspoon white sugar per
   bottle, for priming

1. Steep the black malt and roasted barley in a pan containing 9 cups water at 150 to 160°F for 15 minutes. Putting the grains into a grain bag will make the next step easier . . .

2. Remove the grains and add the liquid malt extract. Bring to a boil until the liquid rapidly foams, then turn the heat down to prevent it boiling over.

3. Break the liquorice stick into three or four pieces and add it to the liquid with the bittering hops. Keep at a steady boil around 45 minutes. 15 minutes before the end of the boil add the aroma hops.

4. Remove the pan from the heat and combine the hot liquid with 9 cups preboiled and cooled water, to help bring the overall temperature down. Give it a good stir to aerate it, and when it has sufficiently cooled to below 75°F strain the liquid into your fermentation vessel of choice. Discard the hops, but rescue the liquorice root pieces and put these back into the bucket. Give it another stir for luck.

5. Pitch the yeast, and place it somewhere warm—around 60 to 75°F is ideal. Fermentation should take 1 to 2 weeks.

6. When fermentation has finished, prime the sterilized bottles with sugar as described in the basic beer recipe (see page 74) before filling them with beer. Make sure the liquorice root gets left behind. This beer is drinkable after 10 days but we recommend waiting a minimum of 3 weeks. And you should certainly set aside at least one bottle for several months to enjoy it at its best.

Making time: 2¼ hours | **Fermenting time:** 1 to 2 weeks | **Maturing time:** 1 week

RASPBERRY ALE

Many years ago, in our youthful beer-drinking prime, if we wanted a fruit beer we had to travel to Belgium to get one. These days they are a little easier to obtain, but will often contain sugary syrups rather than fresh fruit—all the more reason to brew your own. Raspberries are our first-choice fruit for a beer immersion—it preserves their tart flavor well, and they perfectly complement the caramel malt and bitter hop taste of this beer. In fact, this red berry beauty is such a success that everyone who samples it wonders why raspberry ale isn't a more common sight in bars.

3½ cups raspberries
¾ cup crushed crystal malt
1¼ cups liquid malt extract
  (light or amber)
1¾ cups extra light dry
  malt extract
⅓ cup flaked barley
1 small handful of bittering hops
ale or brewer's yeast
½ teaspoon white sugar per
  bottle, for priming

MAKER'S NOTES:
WANT MORE FRUITY FUN?

Why not experiment with some of these natural fruit flavors for your beer? Try cherry, peach, blackcurrant, strawberry, pineapple or plum.

1. Select blemish-free raspberries, wash them and put them in the freezer (this helps them release their juices when thawed).

2. Put the crushed crystal malt into a pan with 9 cups water (they can go in a grain bag if you have one). Heat the water until it reaches 150 to 160°F, then cover with a lid and steep 15 minutes, maintaining this temperature and stirring occasionally.

3. Remove the grains and add the liquid and dry malt extracts and flaked barley—the latter can go into a grain bag if you have one. Bring to a boil until the liquid rapidly foams, then turn the heat down to prevent it boiling over. Add the hops and keep the liquid at a steady boil around 45 minutes.

4. Combine this liquid with 9 cups preboiled and cooled water, to help bring the temperature down. Give it a good stir to aerate it, and when it has sufficiently cooled to below (75°F strain the liquid into your fermentation vessel of choice.

5. Add the yeast according to the instructions on the packet and leave to ferment somewhere warm—60 to 75°F is ideal.

6. After a few days of fermentation the beer should display a large, crusty head of foam. When this dies back down to a thin layer, add the raspberries to the bucket, making sure they're defrosted first, and replace the lid.

7. When fermentation has finished, prime the bottles with sugar as outlined in the basic beer recipe (see page 74). Put the beer somewhere warm 2 days, then leave in a cool place at least 1 week to mature before drinking.

Making time: 2¼ hours | **Fermenting time**: 1 to 2 weeks | **Maturing time**: 2 weeks

VIKING ALE

Did Vikings brew beer? Of course they did. Beerologists are unsure about exactly what would've gone into a Viking's brew, but most agree it would probably have been something like the Finnish drink sahti. This fearsome ale features various grains, including rye, and is filtered through juniper twigs. We've used berries for our juniper dosage, which contributes to some intense sharp and fruity flavors rounded off with a dry, bitter finish. This striking Viking ale is not one for the meek.

¾ cup crushed crystal malt
¾ cup flaked rye
2 cups liquid malt extract
   (light or amber)
1 very small handful of
   bittering hops
⅛ ounce juniper berries
ale or brewer's yeast
½ teaspoon white sugar per
   bottle, for priming

1. Put the crushed crystal malt and flaked rye into a grain bag and drop into a pan with 9 cups water. Heat until it reaches 150 to 160°F. Cover and steep 15 minutes, maintaining this temperature and stirring occasionally.

2. Remove the grains and add the liquid malt extract. Bring to a boil until the liquid rapidly foams, then turn the heat down to prevent it boiling over. Add the hops and keep the liquid at a steady boil around 45 minutes.

3. Gently crush the juniper berries and add these after 30 minutes of boiling, giving them 15 minutes to impart their unique bitter flavors.

4. Remove the pan from the heat, strain the liquid and combine with 9 cups preboiled and cooled water, to help bring the overall temperature down. Give it a good stir to aerate it, and when it has sufficiently cooled to below 75°F strain the liquid into your fermentation vessel of choice.

5. Add the yeast according to the instructions on the packet and leave to ferment somewhere warm 1 to 2 weeks—around 60 to 75°F is ideal.

6. Prime the sterilized bottles with sugar as described in the basic beer recipe (see page 74) before filling them with beer. Put the bottles somewhere warm 2 days, then leave in a cool place 2 weeks to mature before drinking.

Making time: 3 hours | **Fermenting time**: 1 to 2 weeks | **Maturing time**: 1 week

PUMPKIN ALE

America appears to have a national addiction to pumpkin pie—and Americans have even taken to quaffing it in the form of pumpkin ale, a beer laced with the familiar pie spices. It makes a refreshingly spicy brew that's so good it has earned a place in this book. Canned pie mixes are often used, but we prefer to start with the raw ingredients for our take on this unusual ale.

1 small pumpkin (weighing no more than 2¼ pounds), peeled, seeded and flesh chopped into chunks

2¼ cups liquid malt extract (light or amber)

1 small handful of bittering hops

ale or brewer's yeast

½ teaspoon sugar per bottle, for priming

SPICE MIX
½ a cinnamon stick
¾-inch piece gingerroot, peeled and grated
2 cloves
a pinch of grated nutmeg

1. Preheat the oven to 350°F. Spread out the chunks of pumpkin on a baking sheet, and roast until soft—around 1 hour.

2. Stuff the roasted pumpkin into a grain bag and drop into a pan containing 9 cups water. Bring the water to a boil and allow it to simmer, with the lid on, 15 to 20 minutes, stirring occasionally. Remove the grain bag and squeeze as much liquid as possible from the soggy vegetable mass. Discard the pumpkin.

3. Add the liquid malt extract to the pumpkin-flavored water. Bring to a boil until it rapidly foams, then turn the heat down to prevent it boiling over. Add two-thirds of the hops, and keep the liquid at a steady boil around 45 minutes. Add the remaining one-third of the hops for the last 5 minutes of the boil to give an additional hoppy aroma to the beer.

4. Combine the hot, malty liquid with 9 cups preboiled and cooled water, to help bring the overall temperature down. Give it a good stir to aerate it, and when it has sufficiently cooled to below 75°F strain the liquid into your fermentation vessel of choice. Add the yeast according to the packet instructions and leave to ferment somewhere warm—around 60 to 75°F is ideal.

5. During the next few days the beer will develop a crusty head. When this subsides, heat the spices in ½ cup boiling water and simmer 5 minutes. Let cool before straining, then add the flavored liquid to the beer. Let the beer sit to complete fermentation.

6. Prime the sterilized bottles with sugar (see page 74) before filling with beer. Put the bottles somewhere warm 2 days then leave in a cool place at least 1 week to mature before drinking.

PUMPKIN PIONEERS

Pumpkin ale isn't quite the modern novelty as you might think. Early colonists, desperate for some home-comfort beers, would have been disappointed by the lack of barley growing in America so often resorted to the abundant pumpkin to brew with. Albeit without the full-on pie spices.

Making time: 2¼ hours | **Fermenting time**: 1 to 2 weeks | **Maturing time**: 1 week

ENGLISH BROWN ALE

Brown ale, like many beers, varies slightly in style depending on where you are in the world. In England, where this type of beer originates, they are typically dark drinks with a minimum amount of hops playing second fiddle to the beer's maltiness. American-style brown ales have more hops. We've added a richer color and toastier flavor through the addition of a touch of a roasted grain called "chocolate malt"—it's named for its chocolatey color, but might just give you a slight taste of cocoa too.

⅓ cup crushed crystal malt
generous 1 cup liquid malt extract
   (light or amber)
1½ cups dark dry malt extract
2 tablespoons chocolate malt
1 very small handful of hops—
   ideally bittering English hops
   such as Goldings or Fuggles
ale or brewer's yeast
½ teaspoon white sugar per
   bottle, for priming

1. Put the crushed crystal malt into a pan with 9 cups water (if you own a grain bag, pour your crushed malt into that first) and heat until it reaches 150 to 160°F. Cover with a lid and steep 15 minutes, maintaining this temperature and stirring occasionally.

2. Remove the grains and add the liquid and dry malt extracts with the chocolate malt. Bring to a boil until the liquid rapidly foams, then turn the heat down to prevent it boiling over.

3. Add the hops and keep at a steady boil around 45 minutes.

4. Remove the pan from the heat and combine the hot liquid with 9 cups preboiled and cooled water, to help bring the overall temperature down. Give it a good stir to aerate it, and when it has sufficiently cooled to below 75°F strain the liquid into your fermentation vessel of choice.

5. Add the yeast according to the instructions on the packet and leave to ferment somewhere warm—around 60 to 75°F is ideal.

6. When fermentation has finished prime the sterilized bottles with sugar as described in the basic beer recipe (see page 74) before filling them with beer. Put the bottles somewhere warm 2 days, then leave in a cool place at least 1 week to mature before drinking.

GINGER ALE

The interchangeability of the generic names "beer" and "ale" can be bewildering, but put the word "ginger" in front of either and confusion multiplies to the extent of not even knowing if you're dealing with an alcohol or a nonalcohlic drink. All you need to know about this recipe is that (a) it's a proper beer with malt, hops, alcohol and a burst of ginger, and (b) it's terrifically tasty. Think of it as a great pint of bitter with a warming tickle of gingery spice, then sit back, take a large swig and ease away any lingering confusion . . .

scant 1 cup liquid malt extract
 (light or amber)
4-inch piece gingerroot, peeled
 and roughly chopped
generous 1 cup white sugar
juice and zest of 1 unwaxed lemon
1 small handful of bittering hops
ale or brewer's yeast
½ teaspoon white sugar per
 bottle, for priming

1. Heat 9 cups water in a large pan and add the malt extract, stirring until it has dissolved.

2. Roughly chop the ginger and hit it to help release its spicy goodness. Add this to the pan with the sugar and the zest of a lemon (no pith, please).

3. Bring to a boil until the liquid rapidly foams. Turn down the heat to prevent it boiling over, then turn the heat back up and repeat the process until the rapid foaming ceases. Partially cover the pan and keep to a gentle boil 15 minutes, then add the hops.

4. Continue on a gentle boil a further 30 minutes (a total of 45 minutes).

5. Combine this liquid with 9 cups preboiled and cooled water, to help bring the overall temperature down. Give it a good stir to aerate it.

6. When the temperature has cooled to around 75°F, strain the liquid into your fermentation vessel of choice. Squeeze the juice from the lemon into the mixture, pitch the yeast and place somewhere warm.

7. Fermentation will take 1 to 2 weeks, and then it's time to bottle. Prime the sterilized bottles with sugar as described in the basic beer recipe (see page 74) before filling them with beer. Put the bottles somewhere warm 2 days—this will allow the additional sugar to ferment, and will condition the beer and give it a light sparkle—then move them to a cooler spot. Allow at least 1 week for the beer to mature in the bottles before drinking.

SPARKLING DRINKS BASICS

It's brewing in its simplest form—creating a sparkling drink by introducing yeast to a fruity/flowery/vegetable-based sugar solution and allowing the concoction to ferment is the easiest and quickest way to acquaint yourself with the magical art of home brewing.

The recipes in this section go to show that with a bit of imagination and inclination, there are endless fizzy concoctions just waiting to be made. In the hands of an aspiring brewer, a small pack of yeast will take you on your own booze odyssey, which will have you scouring hedgerows, allotments and cupboards in search of potential fermentables.

The simple techniques deployed to make a sparkling drink are utilized in many well-known recipes. You will probably be familiar with everybody's favorite, elderflower "champagne," the fancifully monikered hedgerow booze that shares very little in common with the process of making its French namesake. And, of course, there's ginger beer—the ubiquitous, fizzy, sticky, spicy beverage that's a staple of summer picnics and a magnet for wasps. These are the grandstand tipples—the headline grabbers— but there are countless more to be made and others yet to discover.

SPEEDY BREW
The main pull for the aspiring sparkling drinks maker is the fast turnaround time from raw ingredients to quaffable tipple. The potential is there to create a sparkling sensation within a few days, ideal for impressing guests with your fermenting prowess at barbecues and parties. And even if things don't quite turn out the way you'd planned, mistakes can be rectified and recipes can be adapted within a relatively short space of time. It's also a useful indication of how sugars, acids and different ingredients will complement each other, providing invaluable knowledge for when you start attempting some of the more complex wine, mead and hard cider recipes within this book.

WHAT TO FERMENT?
Generally speaking, punchy fruit flavors work best, but if you like the taste of something, try it and see how it turns out! You'll be selecting the ingredients for flavor alone, so don't worry about the sugar content of what you intend to ferment—your yeast will get all the fuel it needs from the sugar in our recipes.

One point to consider is adding some sharpness to help produce a balanced drink. Unless you are fermenting something super-citrussy, it's advisable to drop in some lemon juice or zest to raise the acidity—just remember, though, that white lemon pith will impart unwanted bitterness, so be careful not to introduce any into the mix.

BOOZE BOMBS

As tempting as it may be to bottle your sparkle in fancy glass bottles, we would advise keeping and serving your drinks in plastic ones. Your sparkling drink will still be fermenting and therefore giving out CO_2, and nothing will spoil a picnic like an exploding bottle of ginger beer. We would also suggest storing your drinks in the refrigerator once fermented, as cold temperatures will inhibit the action of the yeast.

Vinegar is another easy-to-source acid that you may want to introduce. We prefer to use cider vinegar, but any kind will do. It'll give your sparkling plonk a more rounded flavor, but go easy with it.

BASIC EQUIPMENT

Apart from basic kitchen items, such as stirring spoons and straining sieves, the main piece of equipment you will need is a receptacle to ferment your booze in. Simple food-grade buckets are the most obvious choice, as they offer ample space for both large and small quantities of liquid. Don't worry about using a lid; a (clean) dish towel draped over the top will prevent any airborne nasties entering your booze, while also allowing oxygen inside the fermenter, which is needed to start off the process.

HITTING THE SWEET SPOT

Your drink is meant to be consumed while "live," meaning that it is still under fermentation, with the yeast giving out CO_2 as it converts the sugars, thereby providing the sparkle. The skill is finding the "sweet spot"—the point at which there is enough sugar still remaining in the drink to make it pleasantly sweet. And here, of course, lies the trade-off. The more sugar that remains means the less that has been converted to CO_2 and, more crucially, alcohol.

Although our sparkling drinks recipes aren't alcohol free, they are relatively low in strength, designed mainly for their ease of making and for a fast turnaround. There is, of course, a way to raise the alcohol levels if you wish . . . simply increase the sugar content and leave the drink to ferment for longer.

DITCH THE DIRT

One slight drawback in the making of these drinks is that you tend to get some unsightly sediment within the bottles. In wine and hard cider making, you would normally rack the liquid (see page 16) to rectify the problem. Performing this on a sparkling drink will lose you precious CO_2 and will therefore diminish the impact of a foaming champagne flute if an urgent social gathering demands the presence of your fizzy booze.

Fortunately, there is a quick fix. Simply invert the bottle, allow the sediment to gather at the neck, then place underwater and quickly release and reseal the screw cap. The pressure will expel the sediment, leaving you with a clear, sparkling tipple, ready to impress.

Making time: 10 minutes | Fermenting time: 1 day | Maturing time: 4 to 5 days

SIMA (FINNISH SPRING MEAD)

Sima, or "spring mead," is a spritzy Finnish booze, traditionally supped on May 1 during the Vappu festival, a nationwide celebration to mark the joyful arrival of spring and the passing of winter. It's an absolute breeze to make and is ingenious to boot; the inclusion of raisins not only adds depth to the flavor, but they also serve as an indication of the drink's readiness, rising to the surface* when it's ready for quaffing.

juice and zest of 4 unwaxed
    lemons
heaped ½ cup white sugar
heaped ½ cup brown sugar
ale yeast
1 small handful of raisins
2 teaspoons sugar per bottle,
    for priming

1. Boil 8 cups water in the largest pot you can find. Pour the boiling water into a plastic fermenting bucket, then add the lemon zest, lemon juice and sugar. Give it a good stir to dissolve the sugar, then let cool.

2. Add in the yeast, give the mixture another stir, then loosely cover with a dish towel and put the fermenting bucket somewhere warm for a day or so, until bubbles start to form on the surface of the liquid.

3. Strain the liquid through a muslin cloth into two 2-pint plastic carbonated drinks bottles. Add a few raisins and 2 teaspoons of sugar to each bottle, fasten the caps, then put them in the refrigerator.

4. Keep the bottles in the refrigerator 4 to 5 days, remembering to regularly loosen the caps to release the pressure and reduce the chance of explosions. When the raisins in the bottles rise amusingly to the surface, your sima is ready.

5. Open. Drink. Hello sunshine!

VAPPU FESTIVITIES

During Vappu festivities, it is tradition for all Finnish high-school alumni to wear their white, sailor-esque graduation caps. Unofficial custom dictates that all white cap wearers must get as drunk as sailors through copious consumption of sima, fortified with vodka.

Put a flashlight behind your bottle of sima, and voila—you have a low-tech (if slightly disappointing) lava lamp.

Making time: 20 minutes | **Fermenting time**: 2 to 3 days | **Maturing time**: 1 day

TEPACHE

World cuisine has been unkind to the pineapple—it rarely features beyond being dotted over the top of a pizza with processed ham, or canned in overly sweet syrup. Thankfully, Mexicans treat it with a lot more respect, using it to make this quick and easy sparkling drink. Fermentation starts naturally as a result of action from the frisky wild yeasts which reside on the pineapple rind. And, what's more, you don't even need to use the flesh—that can be saved for something else . . . just please don't use it as a pizza topping.

2¼ cups dark brown soft sugar
1 cinnamon stick
the core and rind of 1 very ripe
  pineapple, cut into chunks

1. Put the sugar into a pan with the cinnamon stick and cover with 6 cups water. Mexicans use special piloncilo sugar, but a dark brown soft sugar will work just fine.

2. Bring the water to a boil, then simmer around 5 minutes, stirring to dissolve the sugar. Set aside to cool.

3. Mexicans ferment their tepache in lidded earthenware pots. In the absence of such crockery, use a large glass pitcher or bowl. When the liquid has cooled to blood warmth, remove the cinnamon stick and pour it into your glass vessel. Add the chopped pineapple rind and core and cover with a plate, cloth or plastic wrap.

4. Put the vessel somewhere warm. After a while bubbles will steadily rise to the surface, gradually increasing in frequency. Leave to ferment 2 to 3 days.

5. Strain the tepache into a pitcher, cover with plastic wrap and store in the refrigerator. Drink after 1 day and within 48 hours.

NICK'S TIP
FLESH IT OUT
Stuck for something to do with your pineapple flesh? Besides making our delicious pineapple wine (see page 28) you can blend it into a great smoothie or juice it and add it to cocktails. We suggest you try dropping a few chunks of pineapple into our Spiced Rum (see page 165) and dilute with pineapple juice.

SERVING SUGGESTION
Tepache is a thirst-quenching treat served straight from the refrigerator with ice. We like to give it the full Mexican treatment by rubbing the rim of a glass with a piece of lime and dipping it into a mixture of chili flakes and salt before filling with cold tepache.

Making time: 10 minutes | **Fermenting time**: 7 to 9 days

CANNED FRUIT FIZZ

When the urge to brew is too strong to resist and time is of the essence, we will often shamelessly turn our attentions to the kitchen cupboards and the canned treats that lie within. A can of fruit contains all you need for a successful brew: rich, fruity flavors and fermentable sugars in abundance. Simply add lemon juice to cut through the sweetness, and yeast to start the party. Pass this around at summer picnics, or serve in champagne flutes at cocktail parties; just don't reveal how you made it.

14-oz can of fruit (whatever type of fruit you like)
juice of 1 unwaxed lemon
scant 1 cup granulated sugar
ale yeast

1. Search your cupboards and pull out a can of fruit. It doesn't matter what variety . . . prunes (!) work brilliantly, but cans of peaches, pears or even grapefruit will work just as well. Please make sure you avoid cans of soup.

2. Smash up your chosen fruit with a potato masher or a suitable blunt instrument, then put it in a sterilized fermenting bin, along with the lemon juice and sugar. Boil 8 cups water and add to the fermenting bin, giving the mixture a stir.

3. Once cool, add the ale yeast, cover with a dish towel or loose-fitting lid and leave it somewhere warm to ferment.

4. Allow to ferment 3 to 4 days, then pour the mixture through a muslin cloth into a plastic carbonated drinks bottle.

5. Screw the lid on securely, and leave to ferment a further 4 to 5 days. Release the gas every so often by unscrewing then retightening the lid. Failure to do so may result in explosions and walls dripping with sticky liquid. Not nice.

6. Remember, your fruity brew will continue to ferment in the bottle and will become drier in flavor (and more alcoholic) as time passes.

RICH'S TIP
EXTRA FLAVOR
Try using two cans of fruit if your chosen fizz lacks flavor. Or mix and match flavors for a sparkling fruit salad.

DID YOU KNOW?

The concept of canned food was invented by Nicolas Appert in the 1790s. He won a competition run by French emperor Napoleon Bonaparte, who wanted to find a way of preserving food for his war fleet to consume on their long, marauding overseas voyages.

Making time: 20 minutes | **Fermenting time**: 3 days

FIZZY ICED TEA

Iced tea was born from the 19th-century practice of making cold tea "punches" that were served at raucous high-society gatherings. These green tea beverages were laden with booze to amuse the upper classes, and were often dizzying concoctions of different spirits. Our mild-mannered, sparkling version is more akin to the modern-day booze-free variant, but has the added bonus of being "slightly" alcoholic. We will, of course, avert our eyes if you wish to make it a little stronger.

juice and zest of 2 unwaxed
  lemons
7 strong, black teabags
1 cup white sugar
1 teaspoon ale yeast
ice cubes and lemon slices,
  to serve
mint leaves, to serve (optional)

1. Pour 8 cups water into a large pan, then add the lemon zest and bring to a boil.

2. When boiling point is reached, add the teabags, stir in the sugar and remove the pan from the heat.

3. Let the tea steep at least 5 minutes to achieve a strong brew. Squeeze each bag, then remove the teabags and let the tea cool.

4. With a funnel, pour the tea through a muslin cloth into a 4-pint plastic carbonated drinks bottle.

5. Add the lemon juice and yeast, then fasten the lid and give the bottle a shake.

6. Wait patiently for 3 days, occasionally loosening and retightening the lid to relieve the builtup pressure in the bottle.

7. Put the bottle in a refrigerator to chill 1 hour before serving.

SERVING SUGGESTION
Serve with ice, a slice of lemon and mint leaves if you like.

MAKER'S NOTES:
MINT IMPERIOUS

Quite a few of our recipes utilize mint, and there are all kinds of unusual varieties to choose from—pineapple, ginger, apple (our favorite); there's even a chocolate mint. It's easy to grow, too—just remember to constrain your plants in pots or they'll aggressively run riot over your yard.

Making time: 20 minutes | **Fermenting time:** 5 to 7 days | **Maturing time:** 1 week

ELDERFLOWER SPARKLE

The blooming elder is a joyous sight; its fragrant flowers can be seen beaming from hedgerows in late spring, heralding the summer months with their big white faces full of sunny promise (often at odds with the all-too-familiar slate-gray skies at this time of year). Pick them fresh and use them with gleeful abandonment in this classic foraged fizz; it's a sparkling sunbeam in a glass, even if the weather outside is telling you otherwise.

10 hand-sized blooms of elderflowers (pick them before midday to ensure the flowers are fresh, and shake them to remove traces of insects)
3 cups white sugar
2 tablespoons cider vinegar
juice of 2 unwaxed lemons
champagne or white wine yeast

1. Remove as much stalk from the elderflowers as you can, as this can impart unwanted bitterness to your booze.

2. Boil 8 cups water, pour it into a sterilized bucket and add the sugar. Stir to dissolve the sugar.

3. Add to this 8 cups preboiled and cooled water, the lemon juice, cider vinegar and elderflowers, then stir gently.

4. Once cool, add half a teaspoon of champagne or white wine yeast. (You can skip this step if you like, as the natural yeasts found on the flowers should start the fermentation process after 2 days, but we prefer to play it safe.)

5. Cover with a dish towel or something similar, then wait 5 to 7 days before filtering the liquid through a muslin cloth and into a pair of 4-pint plastic carbonated drinks bottles.

6. Leave about 1 week before consuming, but remember to loosen and retighten the lids daily to release the buildup of gas and prevent explosions.

MAKER'S NOTES:
RESPECT YOUR ELDERS

Don't confuse elderflowers with cow parsley. Elderflowers can be found sprouting from woody hedgerows in springtime, while cow parsley dwells closer to the ground (like a cow). Using the latter will result in a nonjoyous, bitter-tasting brew.

❀ FLOWERS

Increasingly, flowering plants (including weeds!) are being allowed the space to grow in areas of our allotment and yards that were previously set aside for vegetables. Not only do they add a splash of color and provide nectar for the bees, but the ones we grow can also be used in drinks making . . .

FINDING YOUR FLOWERS

There are hundreds of flowers that are edible and can therefore be considered for drinks making (there are also many more that are poisonous, so always make sure you know what varieties are suitable for human consumption). Many are common species cultivated for gardens and borders, but huge numbers—including weeds like the dandelion—grow wild in abundance, just waiting for the right time to be picked. For those less disposed to growing or foraging, a good choice of dried flowers is readily available to the home brewer. Elderflowers and rose petals are sold by an increasing number of homebrew specialists, while others such as heather, lavender and cornflower may be sold by herbalists or apothecaries. You might even be surprised to hear that several floral ingredients can be bought at your local grocery store—some specialist teas, such as chamomile, are made from dried petals, for example; extremely convenient for us home brewers.

USING FLOWERS

Flowers have two obvious benefits in our recipes. First, they can provide the craft drinks maker with unusual and unique flavors—think of lavender as an example of a flavor that is like nothing else. They can make the perfect base for a fragrant wine, and sometimes even the tiniest number of petals can transform an infused drink. Second, their aromas can improve an otherwise nondescript wine or add to the complex bouquet of a well-crafted spirit. There are few drink styles that can't be made using flowers, from a malty beer enriched with heather instead of hops to a classic cocktail lifted by the floral aromas of a homemade vermouth. And with the list of edible flowers being so long, there's plenty of scope to experiment with flower power in your own garden and brewing shed.

PRIZED PETALS
OUR TOP TEN BOOZY BLOOMS

Elderflower: This hedgerow favorite is used in all manner of wines, spirits and hard ciders.

Rose: Introduces an unmistakable luxurious bouquet to a variety of beverages.

Chamomile: Try its calming fragrance in a homemade wine or infusion.

Dandelion: The bright yellow flowers lend a subtle bitter flavor to wines.

Lavender: Use sparingly in infusions to release its highly distinctive perfume and taste.

Heather: A traditional flavoring for beer in Scotland.

Violet: The perfumed petals will be familiar to fans of Parma Violets candies.

Cornflower: Their flavor is delicate, but soaking the petals in spirits will impart a vivid blue color.

Borage (pictured): Drop a whole flower into your next cocktail for some natural color.

Hops: Yes, they're flowers too! See page 81 for more detailed information.

Making time: 30 minutes | **Fermenting time**: 5 to 7 days | **Maturing time**: 4 days

LAVENDER SPARKLE

Lavender is a much underexplored flavor, which is only recently finding favor among chefs and food producers. If you're lucky you might find it working its soothing magic in an ice cream, lending subtle fragrance to a tagine, or even being used as a rub for roast lamb or beef. Lavender's strong aroma and unusual flavor aren't to everyone's taste, but try this as an alternative to French champagne for a drinks reception and you'll soon win plenty of converts.

35 lavender flower heads
1 handful of golden raisins, roughly chopped
2⅔ cups white sugar
2 tablespoons cider vinegar or white wine vinegar
juice and zest of 1 unwaxed lemon
white wine or champagne yeast

1. Try to pick the lavender before the buds have fully opened, as then they will have the greatest concentration of flavored oils, and preferably choose a dry day to gather your harvest. Snip the flower heads from the stalks, shake off any bugs and drop the flowers into a clean, sterilized fermenting bin or bucket.

2. The golden raisins will give the drink a bit more body—add them to the bucket with the sugar, vinegar and lemon juice and zest (avoid the pith).

3. Pour 18 cups boiling water, stirring to dissolve the sugar, then cover and set aside to cool.

4. Once the liquid has cooled sufficiently, add in the yeast. Loosely cover with a lid, dish towel or sheet of aluminum foil and set aside somewhere warm to ferment 5 to 7 days.

5. Strain the liquid and pour it into plastic carbonated drinks bottles. Be sure to release the buildup of gas daily to avoid any explosions.

6. You'll be ready to sample your drink around 4 days after bottling, when it will be sweet and pungent. Its characteristics will change over time; it will gradually become drier and more mellow, and is best consumed within 3 weeks. Refrigerate before serving.

MAKER'S NOTES: ENGLISH OR FRENCH?

The lavender family contains many members, but it's the common English variety, *Lavandula angustifolia*, that tends to be used in cooking. Although also edible, French lavender (*Lavandula stoechus*)—distinguishable by its feathery tips—imparts a more bitter flavor. If you've got one of the many hybrid varieties of lavender, sniff it before committing it to the fermentation bucket—if it smells good enough to drink, then use it!

Making time: 40 minutes | **Fermenting time**: 5 to 6 days | **Maturing time**: 10 days

BOOZY DANDELION SODA

Dandelions are among those weeds that can be impossible to permanently remove from the yard without digging huge clumps out of the ground. And come spring, they seem to delight in showing up any lack of weeding prowess by brazenly flashing their bright yellow blooms for all to see. But now you have the perfect excuse for that poor weeding. For this lightly alcoholic soda, which is based on a historical dandelion beer recipe, you'll need your trowel: it uses the whole plant, from flower to root. And if you really hate weeding, even for the sake of booze, don't worry—this recipe requires surprisingly few plants.

8 cups roughly chopped young dandelion plants
1-inch piece gingerroot, peeled and grated
2¼ cups white sugar
juice of 1 lemon
juice of 1 orange
juice of 1 grapefruit
ale yeast

1. Scrub your dandelion plants (soaking them in water for 1 hour will make this easier), before roughly chopping them. Put the dandelions and ginger into a large pan with 2¼ cups water.

2. Bring the water to a boil and gently simmer 10 to 15 minutes, before straining the hot liquor into a bucket.

3. Top up the liquid with 2¼ cups boiling water. Add the sugar and squeeze over the lemon, orange and grapefruit juice. The juice will give the soda a refreshing aroma and add some fruity sharpness to the dandelions.

4. Stir to dissolve the sugar, and allow to cool before pitching the yeast. (We use ale yeast, but wine yeast would be perfectly acceptable.)

5. Loosely cover with a lid or cloth and set aside to ferment 5 to 6 days.

MAKER'S NOTES: THE DANDELION KING

For homebrewers, the dandelion is perhaps the king of the weeds. Besides this fizzy favorite, the flowers can be used to make a fine wine,* and the leaves have often been used to provide beers with bitterness during times of hop shortage. Some breweries found their substitute dandelion-flavored beers so successful that they continue to produce them on an annual basis.

6. Pour your bubbling booze into bottles. Make sure they're suitable for fizzy liquids—plastic bottles work best—and carefully unscrew and then retighten the lids every day to release the buildup of gas.

7. We think this drink tastes best after 10 days—any earlier and the bitterness can be a touch overpowering. It's best served chilled.

Tradition dictates that flowers for dandelion wine should be picked on April 23, St. George's Day. But don't rely on this date . . . if the sun ain't shining, the flowers won't be out in bloom.

Making time: 20 minutes | **Fermenting time**: 2 days | **Maturing time**: 1 to 2 days

CHILI GINGER BEER

This fearsome fiery fizz is one for folks who crave the tongue-tingling excitement of ginger beer but wish to crank up the heat to dizzier heights. Those with a nervous disposition may want to tame this booze using something milder, but we prefer to anoint our ginger beer with a feisty Scotch Bonnet, seeds and all. Do not be alarmed by the initial mouth-scorching chili blast—the burn is fleeting and will not linger on the palate; the warming notes of ginger will soon take over and caress the pain away.

4-inch piece gingerroot, peeled
  and roughly chopped
juice of 2 lemons
1 cup white sugar
1 chili
ale yeast

1. Put the chopped ginger into a sterilized bucket, then add the lemon juice and sugar.

2. Pour over 8 cups boiling water, and stir.

3. Now comes the fun part—adding the chili. If you want to maximize the heat, chop the chili and cast it all in, seeds and all. However, we would advise taking things cautiously for your first batch by removing the seeds. Daredevils can always ramp up the heat in subsequent brews.

4. Wait until the liquid has cooled, then add in the yeast. Cover the bucket with a dish towel, then leave the fiery liquor to ferment 2 days.

5. Pour the beer through a muslin cloth into a 4-pint plastic drinks bottle, and secure the lid.

6. Leave the bottle 1 to 2 days, remembering to vent the bottle occasionally to release the buildup of gas.

7. Allow the bottle to chill in the refrigerator 1 hour or so before serving.

RICH'S TIP
EXTINGUISHING
THE FLAMES
Made your ginger beer too hot? Need urgent relief from a flaming mouth? Water (and booze) will only spread the burning capsaicin chemicals that are causing the pain, so go for a neutralizing glass of milk. Failing that, try chomping on a cool cucumber.

Making time: 30 minutes | **Fermenting time:** 3 days | **Maturing time:** 1 week

NETTLE BEER

Without even trying, it would appear we are particularly good at growing nettles—one of the perennial weeds against which we've won a few battles but haven't managed to summon the sustained energy required to win the war. However, one person's weed is another forager's harvest, and nettles are one of the wild foodie's favorite free snacks. Whereas many folk will weed out recipes for nettle pies, pestos and even pakoras, we prefer a sting in the ale . . .

2 pounds nettle leaves
zest and juice of 2 unwaxed
   lemons
3 cups (lightly packed)
   demerara sugar
ale or brewer's yeast

1. Pick young leaves toward the top of the nettle plant (thick gloves come in handy for this task), shaking off as many bugs as you can.

2. Wash the leaves, add the lemon zest,and bring to a boil in 18 cups water, or as much as your pan can hold. At this stage the smell is likely to make you wonder why you're doing this, but you only need to persevere with a gentle simmer for 10 minutes.

3. Strain the liquid into a bucket with the sugar, juice from both lemons and any remaining water that didn't fit in the pan. Stir to dissolve the sugar and cover with a lid or dish towel.

4. When the liquid has cooled to room temperature add the yeast, put the cover back on and ferment 3 days before bottling.

5. Carefully distribute the liquid into bottles—the beer will continue to ferment, so use expandable plastic bottles and release the gas regularly. It's ready to drink 1 week after bottling and at its best a few weeks later, but isn't one to keep for any great length of time.

MAKER'S NOTES: EXTRA STING

Nettles have historically been used to give a wild flavor to traditional malt and hop ales, and are occasionally used today by adventurous brewers. If you want to give this recipe more of a bitter, beery taste, add a few hops to the boil. Alternatively, give it an extra sting with the addition of a teaspoon or two of chopped ginger.

SERVING SUGGESTION

Don't expect this to taste like any regular beer, because it doesn't. If you want comparisons, it's probably best treated as a substitute for a cold, refreshing lager but with slightly earthy notes and a definite zesty tang to it. The best description we've heard is "like ginger beer but without the gingery heat." It makes a cheap and fun addition to a summer barbecue, and can be mixed with lemonade or soda water.

LIQUEURS BASICS

Making your own liqueurs is the easiest way of turning a harvest into booze—at its most basic level you're simply adding a flavoring to alcohol, sweetening with sugar . . . and waiting. You don't even need to make the alcohol. Unfortunately, due to the initial outlay on spirits required, this is also likely to be the most expensive booze-making choice, but the final product will be cheaper than a bought liqueur, lasts forever and makes great presents.

Like many people, our first dabble in fusing spirits with food was sloe gin—something we still make every year, comparing one vintage to the next. Regular sloe gin makers will know that the older batches are always the best, a theme that is replicated through most of the recipes—as with a fine whiskey, time gradually mellows the flavors, even when your storage vessel is made of glass rather than oak.

Compare homemade concoctions with store-bought versions and the chances are yours will win hands down—you can get the freshest ingredients, reject the cheap additives and easily tailor each recipe to perfectly suit your palate.

MAIN FLAVORS

If something's edible, the chances are that someone has tried sticking it in a bottle of booze. Fruit, vegetables, leaves, flowers, nuts and even bacon have all had their flavors preserved in alcohol, with varying degrees of success. We have presented a small selection of ideas, but if you get the infusing bug there are millions of possibilities out there—it doesn't take a genius to figure out how to change a recipe for raspberry liqueur into one for blueberries, to give just one example.

SPIRITS

Distilling alcohol at home is illegal in most sensible parts of the world. So for these recipes you'll have to buy your alcohol, which is why we've based them on a standard 70cl bottle. We regularly make half and even third quantities to test out flavor combinations—if you want to make more or less in volume, you'll have to deploy some simple mathematical techniques with the rest of the ingredients.

The spirit you choose as a base for liqueurs and infusions will provide three main functions in the finished drink:

1. It will impart its own flavor.
2. It will extract flavor from the other ingredients.
3. It will make you drunk.

The most commonly used base alcohol is vodka, on account of its having a more neutral taste than the other readily available spirits, but for all our recipes you can interchange the suggested spirit with another of your choice—gin, whiskey, rum, brandy or even that strange-looking bottle of distilled spirit your neighbors brought back from vacation. The stronger the alcohol content, the better the job it will do at extracting the natural flavors from the other ingredients. Most spirits available to

buy fall around the 40 percent volume mark—if you can get your hands on something stronger, you'll probably want to dilute the finished liqueur to make it more drinkable.

Some folk will argue that you need the very best spirits for your infusions, but we don't think the extra expense is necessary, and will usually go for the cheapest bottles of booze we can lay our hands on.

MAKER'S NOTES:
STERILIZING YOUR KIT

Although distilled alcohol does a pretty good job of sterilizing glass bottles and jars, it's best to be on the safe side and prepare your vessels as you would for making preserves. A hot rinse in the dishwasher can be effective. Alternatively, wash and rinse glass in hot water, then dry it out for several minutes in an oven set to around 275°F (238°F for a fan-assisted oven). Always allow the glass to cool before adding cool liquid.

SUGAR

As we've already bought our base booze, we won't need sugar to convert into alcohol—it's used purely to sweeten the finished drink.

When and how to add your sugar is the source of much debate, with some adding theirs at the start of the process while others make a sugar syrup that is added prior to bottling.

With fruit-based spirits, we usually add our sugar at the start of the process—it seems to make sense that all of the ingredients mellow together for the maximum length of time and, with fruit liqueurs, you'll have the bonus of sweet preserved fruit to play with once you've bottled the booze (see individual recipes for ideas). Some purists will argue that adding sugar upfront lessens the alcohol's ability to extract flavor, but we suspect that these benefits are minimal.

However, with ingredients that go straight in the trash after infusing (such as flowers and leaves), or liqueurs that benefit from a reduction in alcohol, we tend to add the sugar later. This is achieved by making a syrup—heating sugar in water until it dissolves, then letting it cool before combining it with the booze.

Standard superfine sugar does the trick of sweetening, and will dissolve after a few days with a bit of agitation. Sometimes, though, you might like to try darker sugars or honey to impart a different flavor.

How much sugar you use depends on how sweet you want your final tipple. Our palates aren't as sweet as some, and so our recipes contain a mid-range amount of sugar. Even if you prefer drinks a touch sweeter, start with a lower amount—it's far easier to sweeten a finished liqueur than to take the sweetness away.

MAKER'S NOTES:
HOW LONG DOES THE INFUSION STAGE LAST?

Some items surrender their flavor to alcohol fairly quickly, while others like to take their time to give you maximum rewards. As a general rule, delicate ingredients such as flowers and soft leaves will give everything up within a few weeks, whereas fruits are worth infusing for 2 to 3 months. Even when strained and bottled, drinks will carry on maturing and improving over time, particularly those containing dark fruits with strong tannins, such as elderberries. If you're desperate to drink your liqueurs early, we don't mind, and suggest sweetening them a touch more to compensate for their lack of maturity.

Making time: 45 minutes | **Infusing time**: 3 months

SLOE (OR BULLACE) GIN

What's the difference between a sloe and a bullace? When it comes to this recipe the answer* doesn't matter—they're perfectly interchangeable and either fruit will give you fantastic results. Sloe (or bullace) gin is arguably the greatest liqueur in the world. These easy instructions produce a drink that, although never quite the same two years running, is always exceptional. And while everyone should try the classic recipe, we've also concocted a few alternatives that use some amazing flavor combinations, regardless of whether you're using sloes or bullaces.

2½ cups sloes or bullaces
1 cup white sugar
1 x 70cl bottle of gin

1. Pick your sloes and bullaces when fully ripe—they should be slightly soft when squeezed rather than hard as bullets.

2. Give them a good wash, then prick their skins in several places to allow the gin to ooze through their flesh and extract the tasty juice. Traditionalists like to while away the hours by steadily performing this task with a sterilized needle. We prefer the rough and tumble of a fork. Alternatively, lazier liqueur makers can freeze the sloes overnight—their skins will crack sufficiently on thawing.

3. Put your pricked sloes, the sugar and the gin into a jar or wide-necked glass bottle, firmly seal the lid and give it a good shake.

4. Put the container out of direct sunlight and leave the gin to work its magic for 3 months. You'll need to shake the jar every day for the first few weeks to make sure the sugar dissolves and encourage the gin to tease out the sloes' flavor. For the remainder of the time an additional agitation every week or two is recommended.

5. When 3 months are up (or longer, if you've forgotten about it) strain the liquid into sterilized bottles. Don't throw away the sugary sloes—they can be used for a second-run sloe whiskey (see opposite), added to hard cider to make a slider (see page 56) or turned into delicious chocolate liqueurs.

6. By all means start sipping on your sloe gin straight away, but it will genuinely continue to improve with age.

MAKER'S NOTES: EXTRA SLOE...

Try something a little different by adding one of these ingredients to your sloe infusion.

Peppercorns: Add a dozen black peppercorns per 70cl bottle to provide your liqueur with some extra warmth for a winter's day.

Grapefruit: For a citric surprise take the zest from half a grapefruit and allow it to infuse with the sloes.

Coffee: There's a Basque tradition that involves soaking sloes, coffee beans and vanilla in aniseed-based spirit to create a drink known as patxaran. We've borrowed the coffee idea for a luxuriously rich version of sloe gin—putting four whole beans into your infusion jar works wonders.

Bullaces are like sloes edging toward damson territory. They're slightly bigger, sweeter and less round than sloes, and their bushes are free of thorns. But as they regularly cross with each other, the boundaries are easily blurred.

Making time: 5 minutes | **Infusing time**: 3 months

SECOND-RUN SLOE WHISKEY

Sloes are nature's gift that keeps on giving. If you've made a batch of sloe gin, the shriveled leftover fruit will still have enough flavor to impart to yet more boozy drinks. Rich likes to plunge the wrinkly fruit into hard cider to make a potent slider (see page 56), whereas Nick prefers to keep the sloe spirit alive with this whiskey infusion. You can deploy any spirit as a base for this sloe bonus, but we think the stronger, malty flavors of whiskey combine perfectly with the delicate tang of second pressing sloe flesh and allow the nutty essence of the stones to showcase their liqueur credentials. You can also substitute the sloes here for second pressing damsons.

fruit from a sloe gin infusion
   (original weight 2½ cups)
1 cup white sugar
1 x 70cl bottle of whiskey

1. Put the strained fruit from your sloe gin back into the jar from which it came. There's no need to rinse off the excess gin; it all adds to the flavor.

2. Add the sugar and whiskey to the jar. Please don't buy an expensive single malt for this recipe—a cheaper blended whiskey will do just fine.

3. Follow the same process as for sloe gin from here on in—shaking regularly at first to dissolve the sugar, then giving it less frequent agitation throughout the infusion period.

4. The whiskey will take on a deep pink tinge, rather than the dense purple hue of sloe gin, and is ready for straining and bottling after 3 months.

SERVING SUGGESTIONS
The charms of this liqueur can be enjoyed straight after bottling, and it is a tipple best served neat. The mellow, nutty notes of the stones can equal any sharpness remaining in the flesh, and come wrapped up in a soothing layer of sweet, oaky goodness. It has become Nick's liqueur of choice to see off a gut-busting pot roast, and is just as wondrous when slowly sipped to ease the soul at the end of a long day.

NICK'S TIP FOR THE CHOCAHOLICS
If one batch of sloe-infused booze is enough for your drinks cabinet, you could use your gin-addled fruits to make a delicious homemade liqueur chocolate. Simply chop the flesh away from the stones, stir into melted chocolate and allow it to reset in the refrigerator.

Making time: 10 minutes | **Infusing time:** 3 months

RASPBERRY & THYME WHISKEY

We love raspberries. Their sharp, fruity flavors enjoy nothing more than being sweetened up with the gift of alcohol—for which they'll reward you with a gloriously tasty, vibrantly red liqueur. Curiously, they're also rather fond of thyme, a herb which will give a subtle depth of flavor to the intense glow of raspberry and the earthy warmth of whiskey. We give our liqueur the merest flicker of thyme and a zesty scrape of orange, but if you're feeling adventurous you can double the herby dose. Or use raspberries on their own to create a thyme-less classic.

around 30 good-sized raspberries, free from blemishes
12 thyme sprigs (each around 2 inches in length)
zest of ½ an orange
⅔ cup white sugar
1 x 70cl bottle of whiskey

1. Wash the raspberries and put them in a jar.

2. Rinse the thyme sprigs and add them to the jar.

3. Add the orange zest to the jar with the sugar and the whiskey. There's no need for an expensive single malt; a cheap bottle of blended whiskey is perfectly suitable.

4. Seal the lid and give it a good shake. Put it in a cool, dark place and let it infuse. The jar should be shaken daily until the sugar has completely dissolved, and then every few weeks until you're ready to bottle.

5. After 2 months of infusing, have a small sip of the drink. This recipe isn't as sweet as most of our liqueurs, so you may wish to add a bit more sugar to bring it up to your preferred level, shaking the jar daily until the new batch of sugar has dissolved.

6. Once the liquid has infused for 3 months, strain into clean bottles and seal them. Although it is ready for drinking immediately, liqueurs with tart fruit and lower sugar levels really do benefit from a longer maturation. Try to save at least some of it for an extra 6 months or more.

MAKER'S NOTES: WHISKEY OR VODKA?

We've had many debates with people over which spirit is best for raspberries—whiskey or vodka? Seeing as the good folk of Scotland will claim they grow the world's best raspberries, we've opted for their spirit in this recipe. If you prefer a pure raspberry liqueur, switch to vodka and omit the thyme and orange—this is a drink that creates a great raspberry Bellini when mixed with sparkling wine.

 **Making time**: 30 minutes | **Infusing time**: 3 months

DAMSON & FENNEL VODKA

Of the many plants that possess an aniseed flavor, fennel is our favorite. It's easy to grow, looks good in the garden with its feathery leaves and yellow flowers, and the seeds, leaves and bulbous root are all edible. We've recruited the seeds for this recipe in a supporting role to the wild, plummy flavors of the damson—they bring out its fruitiness and give the drink a sumptuous, sweet caress of aniseed at the finish.

2½ cups damsons
1 teaspoon dried fennel seeds
1 x 70cl bottle of vodka
1 cup white sugar
6 black peppercorns

1. If you're not lucky enough to have damsons growing wild near you, keep an eye out for their appearance in grocery stores and farmers' markets in the fall. Choose the freshest, ripest-looking specimens you can lay your hands on. Give them a wash and sever their skins with a few well-executed thrusts of a fork on their juicy flesh. Or let the freezer do it for you—the process of freezing and thawing will sufficiently crack their skins.

2. Next, it's time to give the fennel seeds some rough treatment, by lightly cracking them with a mortar and pestle.

3. Put all the ingredients in a jar (you can spare the peppercorns any physical abuse) and seal it with a tight-fitting lid.

4. Give the jar a thorough shake and put it somewhere cool, out of direct sunlight. Shake it daily for 2 weeks, checking to make sure the sugar completely dissolves. The mixture will appreciate being shaken a few more times throughout the infusion process until you're ready to bottle.

5. After a minimum of 3 months' infusing, strain the liquid into bottles. Unless you use all but the finest of straining meshes you'll almost certainly find tiny bits of damson in your deep purple liquid. To remove these give it a second, slower straining through coffee filter paper.

SLOES VS DAMSONS

Many folk will argue that a straight damson vodka is even better than sloe gin—the same piquant plummy flavors, but a much more mellow proposition. If you want to see for yourself, simply omit the fennel from this recipe.

Making time: 30 minutes | **Infusing time**: 3 months

WILD BRANDY

If you're a fan of good port but crave something darker, boozier and more intense, a simple blackberry and brandy infusion is the drink for you. But if you want to crank the intensity up to maximum, this liqueur will send you wild with excitement. Just as the deep, mellow richness of the blackberries seduces your taste buds, along comes a sturdy slap of tart elderberry goodness. Compared to our wild brandy liqueur, port is for wimps.

2½ cups blackberries
1¼ cups elderberries
1 cup white sugar
1 x 70cl bottle of brandy

1. Pick the fattest, ripest, juiciest blackberries and elderberries you can find. The blackberries can be simply washed and put in a large jar, but you'll need to remove the elderberries from their stalks before they join them. Elderberries have a habit of ripening at different times on the same head, so first pick off any young green or old shriveled berries and discard them. The easiest way to strip the ripe fruit from the stalks is with fingers, but if you don't want your hands to look like you've just come from a production of *Sweeney Todd*, flick them off by dragging them through the tines of a fork.

2. Add the sugar and brandy to the jar with the fruit, then firmly seal the lid and give the jar a vigorous shake.

3. In order to preserve the luxuriously deep color of your drink, keep the jar somewhere cool and dark. Shake the jar daily until the sugar has dissolved, and continue to agitate it every week or two throughout the infusion time.

4. This is definitely a drink not to be rushed, so try to hold out 3 months before bottling. Strain the liquid through a fine sieve or mesh—gently press the fruit to remove the last drop of goodness without getting too heavy-handed and making a mess. Small particles of fruit are likely to be drifting through your bottled liquid, although it will be so dark they may not be obvious. If you want to remove these, strain for a second time through coffee filter paper.

5. Wild brandy benefits from aging in the bottles more than most liqueurs, so it's well worth being patient to allow the flavors time to mellow. If you're intending to drink it straight after bottling, you may wish to add a bit more sugar to smooth out the edges.

NOT-SO-WILD BLACKBERRIES
These days you can buy blackberry bushes especially cultivated for growing in the yard. They tend to be free of thorns and often claim to provide bigger fruit.

🫐 BERRIES

Flaunting their many shiny hues, berries scream for attention from hungry—and thirsty—passersby. From sweet, juicy grocery store favorites to unusual, wild, bitter fruits—if it's edible, we'll find a way of turning it into booze. Fresh bought berries can often be expensive and, while cheaper frozen fruit is perfectly acceptable, it's a whole lot more rewarding growing or foraging for your own harvest.

GROWING BERRIES

There are plenty of berry bushes that can be grown easily in the yard, many of which take up little space and thrive with a minimum of care and attention. For beginners, blackcurrants or gooseberries make an ideal choice. Bushes are usually sold in pots or as bare roots to be planted during their dormant season. All you need to do is plant the fruit bush into a freshly dug hole, cover the roots with soil (preferably mixed with a bit of compost or manure), give it a good watering . . . and wait. Depending on how trusting you are of nature, you may wish to protect your crop from greedy birds before they ripen. Most homegrown berries freeze extremely well, so why not stick your surplus harvests in the freezer and combine them with another fruit later in the year for a boozy berry medley.

FORAGING FOR BERRIES

A huge variety of berries growing in the wild can be used as a base for drinks making. Several of our recipes have been chosen because they feature berries local to us—particularly abundant examples are elderberries, blackberries and sloes, and we even know of a secret spot for wild raspberries. If you've got alternative foraging options, get creative by swapping the berries in our recipes for some of your own harvested fruit. Just be sure that you know exactly what you're picking to avoid consuming anything poisonous, and make sure you leave a decent supply of fruit untouched for the wildlife.

BERRY BONANZA
FIVE UNUSUAL BERRIES FOR EXPERIMENTAL BREWS

Japanese wineberry: This perfectly named fruit is familiar to North American foragers. It looks and tastes a bit like a raspberry.

Honeyberry: Does it taste like honey? Er, no. It's an edible variety of honeysuckle and produces fruit that resembles an elongated blueberry, with a similar taste.

Jostaberry: Botanical experts love meddling with berries to produce new species. The jostaberry is one such "invention"; the result of crossing blackcurrant with gooseberry.

Rowan berry (pictured): The fruit of the mountain ash grows with wild plenitude. It's a bitter fruit that can be used in beers and infusions.

Sea buckthorn: These bright orange berries are vigorous growers, whether cultivated or out in the wild, but come well protected by thorns. They have a sour, fruity flavor.

Making time: 40 minutes | **Infusing time**: 2 to 3 months

CRÈME DE CASSIS & KIR ROYALE

Plump, ripe blackcurrants are a treat. If you grow your own, they deserve nothing more than having their sharp, fruity essence preserved in alcohol. And if that isn't good enough for them, the resulting liqueur can be used to make one of the simplest but greatest cocktails around: Kir Royale. Champagne and crème de cassis—like the most luxurious blackcurrant cordial but with bubbles and booze. So, let's start with those blackcurrants . . .

FOR THE CRÈME DE CASSIS
5¾ cups blackcurrants
1⅓ cups vodka
1⅓ cups brandy
10 blackcurrant leaves
scant 2 cups white sugar

FOR THE KIR ROYALE
crème de cassis
champagne

MAKER'S NOTES: FOUR MORE COCKTAIL KIRS

Kir: Without the "Royale" endorsement, a Kir is crème de cassis combined with dry white wine.

Kir Normande: For this tipple, the fizz is provided by sparkling hard cider from the French region of Normandy.

Kir Elder: The champagne is substituted for elderflower fizz.

Kir Impérial: In this cocktail the crème de cassis is set aside, with raspberry liqueur taking its place (you can use our raspberry liqueur on page 120).

1. Pick your blackcurrants at their peak of juiciness. Remove any lingering stalks and the fluffy bits at the other end, then rinse. Alternatively, frozen blackcurrants are acceptable.

2. Rough the currants up with a fork or knife—there's no need for currant carnage, but breaking some of their skins will help.

3. Put the currants into a jar with the vodka, brandy and leaves. Don't fret if you can't get hold of fresh leaves; they simply add a different layer of blackcurrant goodness to the blend. Set aside and allow to infuse for 2 to 3 months.

4. Strain the liquid through a muslin cloth or fine sieve and set aside. Remove and discard the leaves.

5. Blitz the currants to a pulp in a blender.

6. Put the sugar and a scant 1 cup water into a pan, and heat to dissolve the sugar.

7. Add the currant purée to the syrupy water, and continue to heat at a very gentle simmer for 5 minutes.

8. Press the juice through a fine sieve using the back of a spoon to leave behind the dry pulp. Combine this juice with the alcohol set aside earlier, and store in sterilized bottles.

TO MAKE KIR ROYALE . . .

Put a shot of crème de cassis (around 1 tablespoon) into a champagne glass. Carefully fill with champagne (you can use any sparkling wine but, technically, this would be called a Kir Pétillant). Gently stir. Drink.

 **Making time**: 15 minutes | **Infusing time**: 2 months

Use this to make a rhubarb and custard cocktail! See page 170 for the "custard."

RHUBARB & VANILLA LIQUEUR

There can be few better ways of serving freshly cooked rhubarb than with a slosh of sweet, creamy custard: a classic British dessert. We figured it was a combination worth turning into an alcoholic drink. You can find our recipe for egg-nog (the "custard") on page 170, but you can still enjoy this sweet liqueur on its own. And if you prefer an unadulterated hit of rhubarb, simply leave the vanilla and orange out.

2 good-sized sticks, or 4 small sticks, of rhubarb (roughly 9 ounces), chopped into small pieces
1 cup white sugar
1 vanilla pod, sliced lengthwise to expose the seeds
zest of ½ an orange
1 x 70cl bottle of vodka

1. Put the chopped rhubarb in a jar with the sugar, and leave for 24 hours.

2. By now the sugar will have got to work extracting the rhubarb juice, so you can add the rest of the ingredients, including the whole vanilla pod. Cover everything with the vodka.

3. Shake the jar to help dissolve the sugar, and leave it in a cool place away from direct sunlight. You'll probably have to give the jar a few more shakes in the first few days to make sure all the sugar has dissolved.

4. Ideally this mixture needs around 2 months to mature before bottling, and the liqueur will continue to mellow and improve with age once in the bottle.

SERVING SUGGESTIONS

For the perfect rhubarb and custard liqueur, combine with egg-nog at a ratio of three shots of egg-nog to one shot of rhubarb and vanilla liqueur. Alternatively, splash the liqueur into real custard and pour it over the dessert of your choice.

Making time: 10 minutes | **Infusing time**: 1 month

JULIA'S ORANGE WHISKEY

For years Nick's mother, Julia, has made the finest orange liqueur around, bestowing it on friends and family for special occasions. Luckily for us, we've managed to prise the recipe from her grasp. The original instructions are believed to have been sourced from an ancient edition of *Good Housekeeping* magazine, although she has adapted it over the years to reach its current state of perfection. And to help us out even more, she has provided us with some invaluable orange whiskey tips.

juice and zest of 2½ large, sweet oranges
¾ cup golden superfine sugar
1 cinnamon stick
1 star anise
1 x 70cl bottle of whiskey

1. Put the orange zest in a sterilized jar.

2. Add the orange juice with the sugar, cinnamon stick and star anise.

3. Pour in the whiskey and seal the jar. Give it a good shake and put it somewhere cool and dark.

4. Shake the jar for the next few days until all the sugar has dissolved, and allow it to infuse for 1 month, giving it another shake or two during this time.

5. Strain off the whiskey through a muslin cloth or a straining bag and bottle. If you want a clearer liqueur, give the liquid a second, slower straining through a coffee filter paper to remove the tiniest bits of orange.

SERVING SUGGESTIONS

This is a delicious zesty orange tipple in its own right, but it can also be used for cocktails and punches in place of more familiar orange-flavored liqueurs, such as triple sec or curaçao. You can even sink a shot into a mug of cocoa for an extra-special hot chocolate orange.

JULIA'S TIPS
Although any sweet oranges will suffice, Nick's mom prefers to use navel oranges* in her liqueurs. Wash the oranges in warm water first. Not only will this remove any shiny wax coating, but it will also soften them a little, which helps when it comes to squeezing out the juice.

*So-named because the orange would appear to have a belly button. This is in fact a second small orange that grows within the larger fruit as the result of a genetic mutation.

Making time: 20 minutes | **Infusing time**: 2 to 6 weeks

LIMONCELLO

For years limoncello was Italy's best-kept booze secret, but recently the rest of the world has developed a zestful love for this lemony liqueur. Among Italian traditionalists there will be precise methods and ingredients* used, but for the rest of us there are numerous ways to produce this delicious digestif. Our easy instructions allow you to make a pure, sweet limoncello or give it a sour edge. You can also choose between a clear or cloudy appearance.

juice and zest of 5 unwaxed
   lemons
1 x 70cl bottle of vodka
1 cup white sugar

1. Put the lemon zest into a jar with the vodka.

2. Although not traditional, we like our limoncello to have a sour taste. To achieve this, add the juice from the lemons to the mix—the more you add, the sourer the flavor. If you're unsure, you may prefer to split the batch and try both options.

3. Seal the jar and set aside to infuse for around 2 weeks.

4. After this initial infusing time, you're ready to sweeten the liquid with a simple sugar syrup. Put the sugar in a saucepan with ⅔ cup water, then heat gently until the sugar dissolves. If you want your limoncello to be clear, let the syrup cool before adding it to the vodka and lemon zest. For a cloudy drink, pour in the syrup while still warm.

5. If you're eager to drink your lemony treat, you can strain and bottle the limoncello after adding the syrup, although we recommend extending your patience by another 4 weeks. Even after straining through a fine-mesh sieve you'll have lots of small lemon bits floating in the mix—but a second, slow straining through filter paper will remove these.

NICK'S TIP
If you can't find a lemon that hasn't got a shiny wax coating, fear not—it's quite easily removed by scrubbing the lemon under hot water.

SERVING SUGGESTIONS

Limoncello is best enjoyed neat, served ice cold as an after-dinner shot—so store your bottles in the freezer for the best results. It can also be used to give a zesty spike to cocktails and fruit punches, drizzled over ice cream or added to a lemon dessert.

*The town of Sorrento produces Italy's limoncello-making lemon of choice. This is a fruit so prized that it has protected status, meaning no lemon grown outside the town can be called a Sorrento lemon.

Making time: 10 minutes | **Infusing time**: 10 days | **Maturing time**: 1 month

RUCOLINO

Did we mention that some people will put anything in booze to see if it makes a suitable liqueur? And did you imagine that salad leaves would be responsible for one of the more successful booze and food combinations? The salad leaf in question is arugula, recognizable to many as the hot, pungent green stuff that adds some pep to a plain sandwich. Italy* is responsible for rucolino, one of our sweetest liqueurs, which delivers delicious peppery and lemony tones and is served as a digestif. Here's our version of this highly sippable salad-based booze.

1 handful of arugula (around
   30 leaves)
1 x 70cl bottle of vodka
zest of 1 unwaxed lemon
zest of ½ an orange
2 cloves
generous 1 cup white sugar

1. Rinse the arugula leaves under cold water, and drop them into a jar with the vodka.

2. Put the lemon and orange zest into the jar, add two cloves, seal the lid and give it a gentle shake. Put it to one side somewhere cool, away from direct sunlight, for around 10 days.

3. After the infusing time is up, make a sweet syrup by pouring the sugar into a pan and covering with a little water. Gently heat and stir until the sugar has dissolved. Let cool.

4. Strain the infused vodka, combine it with the cooled sugar syrup and pour it into a clean jar or bottles.

5. Allow around another 1 month to mature. We recommend taking a few trial sips during this period to see if the sweetness is to your liking. If you detect any bitter flavors, you may wish to add a touch more sweetness to the drink by making a small batch of syrup and adding it a little at a time until you're fully satisfied with the results.

MAKER'S NOTES:
GROW IT

There are various types of arugula available, some of which can be found in the wild in many parts of the world. It's extremely quick and easy to grow and is a perfect choice for containers if you're short on space. The leaves can be regularly picked throughout its growing cycle, and even the flowers are edible.

*The sweet-toothed natives of Naples are responsible for rucolino. They're also credited with inventing the pizza, a dish that often benefits from a sprinkling of homegrown arugula.

Making time: 20 minutes | **Infusing time**: 2 to 3 weeks

MINT, LIME & LEMONGRASS LIQUEUR

One of the first grow-your-own liqueurs we made was crème de menthe—raiding the herb bed for fresh mint leaves to produce a digestif that tasted far superior to the bright green syrupy liquids found in most restaurants and bars. Giddy with our fresh success, we wondered what would happen if we invited mint's best friends from Asian cooking—lime and lemongrass—to join in the fun. And, guess what? It worked, just as we hoped it would, with the trio of Thai flavors all taking it in turns to tantalize the taste buds with every sweet alcoholic sip.

2 lemongrass sticks
zest of 3 limes
1 x 70cl bottle of vodka
a handful of fresh mint leaves
generous 1 cup white sugar

1. Strike the two lemongrass sticks with something hefty to thoroughly bruise them.

2. Drop the lime zest and lemongrass into a jar, and cover with the vodka. Seal the jar, shake and set aside for 2 weeks, giving it a few more shakes in the meantime.

3. Wash the mint leaves thoroughly before treating them roughly—rip and scrunch them with your fingers—as this will help release their minty flavors.

4. Add the mint to the vodka, lime and lemongrass, reseal the jar, give it another good shake and then wait another 2 days.

5. Make a simple syrup by gently heating the sugar and 1⅓ cups water in a pan, stirring until the sugar has dissolved. Let cool.

6. Strain the flavored vodka and combine it with the syrup. Have a taste—if you would prefer it sweeter, make a bit more syrup and add it until your taste buds are content. Bottle and start using straight away.

SERVING SUGGESTIONS

This makes for a good digestif—perhaps after a hot, spicy Thai meal. We also like to combine it with soda water, ice and fresh mint leaves for an Asian-inspired mojito. (If you like the sound of this but disapprove of the use of vodka in a mojito, try substituting white rum in the recipe.)

MAKER'S NOTES: CRÈME DE MENTHE

If you want a simple crème de menthe without the additional flavors, simply start the process at Step 3 and ignore the words "lime" and "lemongrass" in Step 4.

 **Making time:** 20 minutes | **Infusing time:** 2 to 3 months

BEECH LEAF & HONEY LIQUEUR

The beech leaf is an ingredient that perfectly illustrates the magic of alcoholic drinks making. To sniff or nibble a raw leaf gives you no indication of the transformation that takes place once it has been dropped in a bottle of booze—a mysterious nutty flavor develops after just a few weeks of maceration. "Beech leaf noyau" (see box) had a spell of popularity during the 1970s thanks to the book *Food for Free* by Richard Mabey. With the recent rise in popularity of foraging, and the abundance and ease of identification of beech leaves, the drink is having something of a revival, with Mabey's recipe being widely touted once again. As with all infusions, there are many ways to make this drink—we first made ours with white rum (Mabey uses gin and brandy) and we've also laced it with honey to complement the nutty taste.

2 cups young beech leaves
1 x 70cl bottle of white rum
    or vodka
5¾ ounces runny honey

1. Pick beech leaves while they're still young, with a bright lime-green color and a soft, floppy feel to them. The precise volume is not essential—you need enough to roughly occupy two-thirds of the volume of booze when lightly packed.

2. Wash the leaves, shake them dry and pack them into a jar.

3. Pour in the rum or vodka, seal the jar and leave it in a cool, dark place for 2 weeks.

4. Strain the liquid into another jar or bottle, gently pressing the leaves to extract the last few drops of liquid.

5. Add the honey, giving the jar a good shake to help it dissolve. It may take a few days of occasional shaking to fully dissolve. Alternatively you could gently heat the honey with a few tablespoons of water to help it on its way before adding it to the beechy booze.

6. Leave another 2 months before drinking.

MAKER'S NOTES: NOYAU—NUTS OR NOT?

A true noyau (or noyaux) is a liqueur made by infusing nuts or fruit kernels in brandy, with the most famous French versions using a combination of almond and apricot pits. Beech leaf infusions are often referred to as "noyau" on account of the liqueur's nutty notes.

SERVING SUGGESTIONS

The herby, nutty flavors of this liqueur are good for slow sipping when poured over ice, or it can used as a crème de noyau substitute in cocktails.

MAYFLOWER BRANDY

The flower of the common hawthorn does most of its blooming in May. And where we live there's no blossom more abundant than the mayflower. So no one really notices when we deprive the hedgerows of a bagful of hawthorn branches for a brandy maceration. The mild flavor of the mayflower somehow manages to enhance the brandy's fruitiness with additional floral, savory notes. A very pleasant tipple, and a liquid ode to the marvelous month of May.

roughly 2 cups hawthorn flowers
  and leaves
1 cup white sugar
1 x 70cl bottle of brandy

1. Gather a bagful of hawthorn branches containing both flowers and leaves. Sit down . . . and start plucking. For this recipe you need a roughly equal volume of flowers and leaves, but precise amounts aren't important. Gently remove the petals and leaves, putting them in a sterilized jar—this is a job that seems like it'll take forever when you start, but once you get into a relaxing rhythm time soon flies by.

2. Add the sugar to the jar and cover with the brandy. Cheap brandy is fine to use.

3. Seal the jar and give it a good shake, followed by a few more shakes over the next few days to dissolve the sugar.

4. Set aside to let the flavors infuse for 2 to 3 weeks.

5. Strain the brandy into bottles. If you can wait at least 2 months before drinking, you'll be rewarded with a mellower liqueur.

MAKER'S NOTES:
HAW LIQUEUR

You may also wish to consider the hawthorn's fruit (the haw) for a liqueur. Try following our sloe gin recipe (see page 118), using haws instead of sloes—although you should probably resort to a more aggressive method of breaking their skins than painstakingly prodding each one with a fork.

Making time: 25 minutes

IRISH CREAM LIQUEUR

Whenever we serve up this creamy liqueur to one of our friends, we can usually be sure to receive one of three responses: "Wow, it tastes even better than the stuff I can buy," "I didn't realize it was so easy to make" or "I demand some more." Its Irish name comes from the use of Irish whiskey, but we promise not to tell anyone if you substitute with whiskey from somewhere else . . .

2 heaped teaspoons cocoa powder
½ mug of freshly made black coffee (around ¼ cup)
1 vanilla bean (or ½ teaspoon vanilla extract)
½ teaspoon almond extract
1 can (14-oz) sweetened condensed milk
1 cup Irish whiskey (or other whiskey)

1. Stir the cocoa powder into half a cup of freshly made black coffee.

2. Split the vanilla bean lengthwise and scrape the seeds into the coffee. Add the bean too. (Or add the vanilla extract at this point, if using.)

3. Drop the almond extract into the cup and let cool.

4. Strain the coffee into a bowl with the condensed milk and whiskey. Mix it together thoroughly with a whisk or blender.

5. Pour into bottles and store in the refrigerator. You may notice that over time some of the ingredients start to separate. Fear not! A quick shake should soon restore the drink to its blended state. This liqueur is best consumed within 2 weeks.

SERVING SUGGESTIONS
This magnificent milky mélange is delicious on its own, but it can also be used to pep up a mug of coffee or chai tea.

RICH'S TIP
CREAMY NUTS
Almond is the standard nut flavor of choice for Irish cream liqueur, but you don't have to follow the rules. Try coconut extract instead for a tropical take on this recipe.

 **Making time**: 45 minutes | **Infusing time**: 2 to 3 weeks

COCONUT LIQUEUR

Banish all thoughts of the sickly-sweet commercial efforts* that lurk on the grocery store shelves; our homebrewed version is a nutty, creamy, tropical treat that deserves a front-row place in your (rapidly burgeoning) drinks cabinet. Coconuts can be tricky to source, but they are worth your persistence; shy away from the ones found at fairground stalls, however . . . these are often as rotten as the other prizes on offer.

1 ripe coconut
1 x 70cl bottle of white rum
½ a vanilla bean, split lengthwise
1 cup white sugar

1. Choose your coconut and give it a shake. The sound of water sloshing around inside indicates a fresh specimen.

2. Crack your nut. There are various methods of doing this, but we've found that a sharp blow with a spade is an effective, if unhygienic, method. You may prefer to put the nut in a plastic bag and whack it with a hammer.

3. Chop up the coconut meat into bite-size pieces. A sharp, rounded knife is best for this. Watch your fingers, though.

4. Put the coconut meat into a jar, then pour over the rum. Don't waste an expensive bottle; a cheap white rum will do.

5. Add the halved vanilla bean to the jar, seeds and all.

6. Pour in the white sugar and give the mixture a stir.

7. Fasten the lid, then leave the mixture to infuse 2 to 3 weeks, giving it the occasional shake.

8. Strain the liquid twice through a piece of muslin or a coffee filter paper to remove any coconut pieces, then bottle it.

9. Pour. Drink. Merengue!

FACE-PALM
Portuguese explorers were the first to give the coconut its name. The hairy-shelled nut reminded them of the mythical, pumpkin-headed ghoul El Coca, devourer of naughty children and an all-round bad guy.

*You know which ones we mean . . . the ones where you don't know whether to drink them or smear them all over your body as suntan lotion.

CLASSIC COCKTAILS & CURIOS BASICS

Fasten your seatbelts, because it's time to embark on a global booze cruise. On this journey of discovery we'll be introducing you to some curious concoctions, dabbling with strange local customs and showing you how to give a new twist to some familiar classics . . .

The world is awash with booze. Travel to most countries and you'll be able to experience a myriad of local concoctions, many of which are intrinsically linked to the culture and history of that location, and are often taken as part of some social ritual. But while travel has allowed us to experience these strange brews first-hand, as with other forms of cuisine, alcohol taste preferences aren't always universal—a drink that is loved in one part of the world might not be appreciated elsewhere. These preferences for certain tastes are often a result of the ingredients available in a particular location—it can be amazing how humans acquire tastes for certain flavors when choice is limited, particularly when the ultimate objective is to experience the giddy effects of booze.

Taste can also develop for more random social and cultural reasons. Take, for example, absinthe. Originating in 18th-century Switzerland, it is to many people an uninspiring bitter drink, too potent to enjoy on its own and too overpowering to combine with anything else. Yet, to artists and philosophers of late 19th-century France, it became a rite of passage and a way of inducing creativity (albeit with a few self-destructive, hallucinogenic side-effects thrown in). As absinthe's notoriety spread, it started receiving banning orders, thus adding to its intrigue and desirability.

A great benefit of living in modern times is that many of these previously mysterious global drinks, absinthe included, are now easy to replicate wherever you are in the world. Ingredients are no longer confined to their country of origin and, the more of them we get to experience, the more our palates happily accept unusual flavors. So, in the final section of the book, we travel the world on a booze odyssey, playing with numerous drinks-making techniques and experimenting with a wide range of flavors.

We'll introduce you to some drinks you might never have heard of, recreate others that you might have assumed were beyond the means of the home cook, and provide our own variations on some international classics.

A NOTE ABOUT INGREDIENTS

Throughout this book we've been keen to emphasize that quantities often don't need to be exact, and nowhere does that ring truer than in this chapter. If you're not certain you can get your hands on one particular ingredient, try substituting it with something similar. Several of these recipes have been arrived at by us not

WHAT WILL I NEED TO MAKE THESE RECIPES?

Basic kitchen equipment is all you'll need for most of these recipes, as well as suitable containers in which to store your bounty. There's a lot more infusing, plenty of mixing and more than a dash of magic. As with the rest of the book, a clean, sterile environment is important. Occasionally specialist equipment is suggested—either as a mixing container or for serving purposes—but no one will mind if you use a standard crock in place of a German rumtopf pot, and you're welcome to serve your martini in a teacup if you don't have a traditional cocktail glass.

having quite the same ingredients to hand as our Continental friends—so it's up to you to experiment and make your own unique recipes, using ours as a guide.

CREATING YOUR OWN COCKTAILS

Cocktails are simply a combination of various drinks, usually invented for a particular bar, special occasion or famed imbiber at some point in time. Some have become classics and are drunk in high volumes the world over; others are made and then immediately forgotten. Try not to be fooled into thinking that you need to be an expert mixologist to create your own cocktail. While it's true that the very best cocktail makers mix, shake and pour drinks that seem a cut above the norm, there's no reason why anyone can't conjure up a perfect glass of something special. We've included our takes on some classic cocktail recipes and thrown in a few others we've stumbled over somehow or other. Use these recipes to impress your friends with your own customized versions of your favorite cocktail.

GROWING YOUR OWN DRINKS

If you like these recipes, you might want to consider creating your own cocktail garden. Whereas wines usually require large quantities of single foods, most of these recipes feature mere pinches of ingredients, many of which can be grown at home. Base your growing scheme around a few of the key ingredients mentioned elsewhere in the book—such as herbs including mint, fennel, thyme and wormwood (pictured). Add a dash of color with a few flowers—lavender, borage or perhaps a rose. You could even include a few vegetables—if your yard gets a bit of sunshine, chilis and cucumbers are worth growing for their respective heat-giving and cooling properties. Then try adding some more unusual plants to get creative—and here are three suggestions that might inspire. The herb lemon verbena, as its name suggests, has a lemony flavor—making it a useful option for infusions and cocktails. Anise hyssop is a member of the mint family but has a sweet, anise flavor—an interesting substitute for the familiar mint garnish. Alpine strawberries are plants that will happily grow in among other plants, and their tiny, deep-red fruits can pep up a punch. But they're just our suggestions . . . now it's your turn to get creative!

 **Making time**: 5 minutes

SUMMER CUP

A summer cup (aka a "fruit cup") is a centuries-old, boozy, fruity English cocktail. The most famous version is the recipe devised by James Pimm in 1823, which has since become a staple of British summer sporting events. The drink is a combination of vermouth, gin and liqueurs, served diluted with a soft drink and stuffed with fruit. Our version uses beverages featured elsewhere in this book, making it the perfect summer showcase for your booze-making talents.

⅓ cup gin
⅓ cup sweet vermouth
¼ cup orange liqueur
2 tablespoons sloe gin

TO SERVE
orange
lemon
cucumber
strawberries
mint leaves
around 2 cups lemonade

MAKER'S NOTES: MIX AND MATCH

› Try a burst of port or our cherry fortified wine (see opposite) instead of sloe gin.

› Go for a lemony version, with limoncello (see page 132) in place of the orange liqueur.

› Try ginger beer in place of lemonade, or even our chili ginger beer on page 112.

› Add a couple of drops of orange bitters (see page 155).

› For a fancy touch, dot a few borage flowers into each serving.

1. Mix together the gin, sweet vermouth, orange liqueur and sloe gin. Cointreau is a suitable commercially available orange liqueur, but we like to use our homemade orange whiskey (see page 130). For other alternatives see the Maker's Notes, below.

2. You have now made your own summer cup, which will be even better than those you can buy in the store. Easy, huh? To know how to serve it, read on . . .

SERVING INSTRUCTIONS

3. Thinly slice the orange, lemon and cucumber. Folk like to get at least one piece of each fruit in their glass, so cut more slices than the required number of servings. You should get between 8 and 12 generous glasses out of this, but you could eke it out farther if you want to be less liberal with your booze.

4. Take a handful of strawberries and cut them into halves. Put all the fruit into a large pitcher with a handful of fresh mint leaves.

5. Add plenty of ice to the pitcher, then pour in your summer cup and lemonade. We think twice as much lemonade as alcohol is ideal, but you can dilute the drink further with more lemonade.

6. Give the drink a gentle stir, and serve.

Making time: 40 minutes | Infusing time: 1 day

CHERRY FORTIFIED WINE

Some sweet fortified wines, such as port, are made by adding brandy to wine before it has finished fermenting—the extra dose of alcohol kills off the yeast, thus stopping the fermentation process before all the sugar has been converted, resulting in a stronger, sweeter drink. However, it's perfectly acceptable to fortify an already bottled wine, sweeten it with sugar and, while you're at it, add another flavor to the boozy equation. Fat, juicy cherries can take a bottle of red wine to new, luxurious levels—you could try this recipe with your own elderberry wine, but we believe even the plainest bottle of red can be transformed into a fortified favorite.

3 cups ripe, sweet cherries, rinsed and chopped (include the stones and a few stalks)*
1 x 75cl bottle of red wine
½ cup white sugar
⅔ cup brandy

1. Put the chopped cherries in a large jar.

2. Pour the bottle of wine into the jar with the cherries, seal and leave 24 hours.

3. Empty the contents of the jar into a pan with the sugar. Gently heat around 10 minutes to dissolve the sugar and soften the cherries. Stir with a wooden spoon throughout, pressing the cherry pieces against the side of the pan to help them release their juices.

4. Allow the liquid to cool, then strain it into a clean jar through a muslin cloth or straining bag. Firmly squeeze to extract as much juice as possible, leaving behind stones, stalks and unyielding bits of cherry pulp.

5. Add the brandy to the cherry-infused wine and seal the jar, or decant into clean, sterilized bottles.

6. Store in the refrigerator or a cool cupboard, and consume the sumptuous, velvety cherry fortified wine after 1 day and within 1 week.

SWEET OR SOUR

The most commonly available cherries are either sweet (great for eating raw) or sour (usually used in cooking). You can use either, although we prefer the sweeter varieties in this recipe.

*Dried cherry stalks can be used to make a tea that apparently has detoxifying properties—perfect for the morning after indulging in cherry fortified wine.

Making time: 20 minutes | **Chilling time**: 1 hour

RICH'S SANGRI-AHHHHHH

You can be forgiven for dismissing sangria as the quintessential, watery vacation cocktail, and a source of solace for those suffering with their sunburn. For astute booze-ologists like you and I, though, it's a potent, infinitely customizable fruit salad in a glass that pulls ingredients from the four corners of the allotment. Drink with ice and a slice of lemon when the sun is shining . . . dancing around the backyard is encouraged, but not compulsory.

1 x 75cl bottle of red wine
¼ cup brandy
⅔ cup sugar (see box)
5 teaspoons orange liqueur
½ an unwaxed lemon, washed
   and sliced
1 orange, washed and sliced
heaped 1 cup washed and
   sliced strawberries
1 apple, washed and sliced
a few arugula leaves
a few basil leaves, to serve

1. Pour the red wine into a 2-pint pitcher.

2. Add the brandy, sugar syrup (see box) and orange liqueur and stir. You could also add a few drops of orange bitters for an extra orange kick (see page 155).

3. Add all the sliced fruit to the pitcher (reserve a few slices of lemon).

4. Add the arugula leaves—they will pep up the strawberries, intensifying their flavor. Also: it looks good.

5. Put the pitcher in a refrigerator to chill at least an hour before serving with ice, slices of lemon and a couple of basil leaves per glass for good measure.

SERVING SUGGESTIONS

Drinking neat sangria in the sunshine will soon send the imbiber giddy-headed, so dilute to taste with soda water. For those with a sweeter tooth, dilute with lemonade.

MAKER'S NOTES:
SWEET SUCCESS

To blend the sugar successfully into your sangria (or any other cocktail, for that matter), make a simple sugar syrup to avoid any undissolved sugar spoiling your booze. Use a ratio of 1 part sugar to 1 part water, and heat gently until the sugar dissolves. Set aside and add to your mix once cool.

Making time (for the vodka): 15 minutes | Infusing time (for the vodka): 1 week
Making time (for the tomato juice): 45 minutes

BLOODY MARY

Like a good bloody Mary? Want to create a bloody Mary packed with maximum flavor and designed to perfectly suit your own taste preferences? Pick your favorite ingredients from our tomato-friendly list below, and get infusing for spectacular, spicy results. Our favorite tried-and-tested combo uses chilies, mustard, cilantro and bay. Now it's time to discover yours . . .

1 x 70cl bottle of vodka

MIX 'N' MATCH INFUSION OPTIONS
2 whole chilis
a thumb-sized piece of
   horseradish root
1 teaspoon mustard seeds
6 black peppercorns
2 bay leaves
1 handful of fresh herbs (basil,
   parsley or cilantro)

FOR THE TOMATO JUICE
2 pounds ripe tomatoes,
   roughly chopped
2 cups water
½ an onion
1 tablespoon sugar
1 teaspoon salt
1 celery stick

TO SERVE
Worcestershire sauce, to taste
Tabasco sauce, to taste
juice of 1 lemon
a pinch of salt

INFUSE THE VODKA

1. Choose your flavors from the mix 'n' match options, and put them in a jar along with the vodka. If you're using chilis, make a few cuts with a sharp knife to allow the vodka to flow through their innards and draw out the heat. Horseradish advocates should peel their piece of root before adding in one or two pieces.

2. When all of your chosen ingredients have been added to the jar, shake it and set aside 1 week, giving the jar a few more shakes during this time.

3. After 1 week strain the liquid into a clean bottle or jar, and store it in the refrigerator. Now get to work on the tomato juice . . .

MAKE THE JUICE

4. Select ripe and juicy tomatoes. Don't worry about mixing different varieties; your bloody Mary will taste better for it.

5. Put the chopped tomatoes, along with the other tomato juice ingredients, into a saucepan and bring to a simmer.

6. Cover and simmer 25 minutes, then force the mixture through a sieve and let cool.

7. Combine your infused vodka, fresh tomato juice and a pinch of salt in a glass and top with ice. You can continue to build the flavor by adding a dash of Worcestershire sauce, a drop of Tabasco and a squirt of lemon juice.

DRINKING TIMES

Your infused vodka will keep for repeated servings, but the tomato juice will need to be consumed within 2 days.

Making time: Indefinite | **Infusing time**: Minimum 4 weeks

RUMTOPF

If you've never tried a rumtopf before, you're in for a super boozy food treat. This German and Danish tradition involves the routine filling of a jar with seasonal fruits, sugar and rum throughout the year until a special occasion (usually Christmas) warrants its unveiling. The resulting fruity mélange is a celebration of the year's harvest, and serves as both dessert and digestif rolled into one.

assorted fruit
white sugar
dark rum
(see Step 3 for quantities)

IDEAL FRUITS
strawberries, raspberries, cherries,
   currants, apricots, peaches,
   plums, figs, seedless grapes,
   pineapple, kiwis, pears, etc.

FRUITS TO AVOID
anything too soft (such as
   bananas) or too hard (like apples)
   can create a less pleasing texture
   in the mix. The bitterness of
   citrus fruits can overwhelm the
   flavor, while very dark fruits
   (such as blackberries) can
   dominate the color.

1. A traditional rumtopf would be made in a huge earthenware pot specifically designed for the purpose. If you don't possess one, a large jar will suffice. Give your vessel of choice a thorough clean, and you're ready to begin.

2. Decide on the first seasonal fruit to enter the pot. Wash and prepare it as you would for a fruit salad: use only the most pristine pieces and remove any stones, stalks or unwanted skin. Chop larger items into bite-size chunks.

3. Weigh the fruit and drop it into the pot, before adding sugar measured to half the weight of the fruit. (So, if your batch of fruit weighs 10½ ounces, you'll need 5½ ounces or ⅔ cup sugar.)

4. Pour rum over the fruit until it's totally covered. Seal the pot and put it in a dark place until your next batch of fruit is ready.

5. Repeat the process throughout the year with whatever fruit becomes available—measuring out half quantities of sugar to fruit each time and topping up with rum.

6. The last batch of ingredients to enter the jar should do so at least 4 weeks before serving to allow their flavors ample time to join the fruity party.

SERVING SUGGESTIONS
Ladle the fruit and rum mixture into a bowl and enjoy it on its own, with a scoop of cream or poured over another dessert. For a hot-and-cold version, strain off the liquid and gently heat it in a pan before reuniting it with the fruit.

NICK'S TIP
DRINK ME!
If you choose to serve only the fruit for dessert, you can save the infused rum to drink separately—perhaps in a glass of sparkling wine for a fruity rum fizz.

Making time: 45 minutes | **Infusing time**: 2 weeks

ORANGE BITTERS

Bitters are the mixologist's secret weapon: just a few drops added to a simple gin and tonic or fancy cocktail can take its quaffability to another dimension. One of the most popular flavors for bitters comes from the peel of Seville oranges, the citrus fruit that so excites marmalade makers. Not the exclusive preserve of the cocktail maker, a dash of this golden-orange elixir can be used elsewhere in the kitchen; try adding its zesty goodness to marinades, gravies and sauces.

4 Seville oranges
3 cardamom pods
½ teaspoon caraway seeds
½ teaspoon coriander seeds
scant 1 cup vodka

1. Peel the oranges. Unlike other recipes in this book, it's good to include some pith with the zest, as this will increase the bitterness of the end result. Cut the peel into strips and lay it out on a baking sheet, pith side up.

2. Bake in a moderately hot oven (around 275°F) until the peel curls and dries out. This should take around 25 minutes, but make sure you check regularly as it never seems to take the same time twice (we guess this depends on the dryness of the original oranges, thickness of peel and so on).

3. Let the peel cool before smashing it into small pieces with a mortar and pestle or a rolling pin. Don't get too carried away— if all the peel turns to dust it'll take ages to strain it out later. Transfer the broken peel into a jar and pop the trio of spices into your mortar and pestle. Give these a cursory whack to break them up a bit, and tip into the jar with the dried peel.

4. Add the vodka so it covers the dried ingredients, seal the jar and set aside 2 weeks, shaking occasionally.

MAKER'S NOTES:
FIRST WE TAKE MANHATTAN

Want to know what to make with your orange bitters? How about the classic Manhattan cocktail? Simply combine ¼ cup bourbon or rye whiskey with 1 tablespoon sweet vermouth and 2 dashes of orange bitters. Stir together with a few ice cubes and, for a traditional touch, garnish with a maraschino cherry.

5. Filter through a muslin cloth or fine sieve, squeezing out as much bitter booze as you can. It's not necessary to get rid of every last zesty grain, but if you prefer the aesthetics of a clear drink, give it a secondary filtering.

6. Bottle the liquid and experiment by adding a few drops to your next cocktail.

ALTERNATIVELY . . .
Fallen asleep while baking? Fear not! Slightly burnt peel can also be used, and will give the drink additional caramel flavors.

Making time: 15 minutes | **Infusing time**: 2 weeks

SPRUCE BITTERS & SPRUCE MARTINI

Spruce is a centuries-old foraged ingredient that is rather underused today. The needles are packed with vitamin C, which inspired Captain Cook to use them in beer to help his crew fend off scurvy,* but we think we've discovered a better way to enjoy their woodland essence. It's the young, bright-green spruce tips that tend to get the approval of recipe revivalists—they can be eaten raw or even pickled—but you don't need to use the new spring growth in this recipe. The finished beverage can be used a few drops at a time to spruce up martinis with a distinctive scent of the forest.

1 tablespoon spruce needles (see method for preparation)
½ teaspoon coriander seeds, gently cracked
2 allspice berries, gently cracked
4 juniper berries
scant 1 cup vodka

FOR THE SPRUCE MARTINI
⅓ cup gin or vodka
1 tablespoon dry vermouth
2 dashes of spruce bitters

1. Snip a few twigs from a spruce tree. If you're using your Christmas tree, check its provenance first to make sure it hasn't been sprayed with chemicals.

2. Rinse the twigs under water and pat dry. Pluck the needles from the branch (or cut them off with scissors). Measure out around 1 tablespoon of needles and gently bruise them with a mortar and pestle so that they start to release their oily liquid. Scrape them into a jar.

3. Put the coriander seeds and allspice berries into the jar with the bruised needles and juniper berries, and cover with the vodka.

4. Give the jar a shake and set aside 2 weeks, giving it a few more shakes in the meantime.

5. Filter through a muslin cloth or fine sieve, and bottle.

MAKER'S NOTES: SPRUCE OR PINE?

All varieties of spruce and pine can be used, and each will impart a slightly different flavor, but generally we've found pine to be less successful. To tell the difference, spruce needles have four sides and can be rolled between the fingers, whereas pine needles are flatter and don't roll easily. Whatever you do, please avoid the similar-looking yew, as it's poisonous.

FOR A SPRUCE MARTINI . . .

Decide whether you're going to use gin (for the traditionalist) or vodka (for the modernist) and pour it into a cocktail shaker or jar with the vermouth, spruce bitters and a handful of ice. Shake and strain into a glass. Cocktail connoisseurs will most likely garnish their martinis with an olive or a twist of lemon peel. For this recipe we would like to suggest that you use a spruce tip.

*We've tried an approximation of his recipe. It's awful.

Making time: 25 minutes | **Infusing time**: 1 day (overnight)

VERMOUTH

Vermouth, the king of cocktail mixers, is simply a fortified wine that has been flavored and aromatized by any number of botanicals. Despite its flavor complexity, a good vermouth is remarkably easy to make. The recipe below is our own tried and tested version with relatively delicate flavoring, but the real fun in this drink comes from playing around with pinches of your own favorite herbs and spices to create something unique. To extend your choice it can be made using red, white or rosé wine, and can be dry or sweet. It's useful for masking the flavor of a wine that isn't up to scratch—perhaps a bottle of homemade wine that has been opened prematurely.

a pinch of dried wormwood
2 juniper berries
3 pinches of dried orange peel
3 cloves
3 cardamom pods, cracked
6 coriander seeds
2 pinches of dried chamomile
 (from a chamomile teabag)
1 bay leaf
1 star anise
1 x 75cl bottle of red or
 white wine
 ½ cup brandy

FOR SWEET VERMOUTH
¼ cup white sugar

MAKER'S NOTES:
ALTERNATIVE FLAVORINGS

Don't like (or can't find) any of the ingredients in our recipe? Try these:

• Angelica • Burdock root • Cinnamon • Elderflower • Fennel seeds • Gentian root • Ginger • Hyssop • Lavender • Liquorice root • Mace • Nutmeg • Oregano • Peppercorns • Raspberry leaf • Rosemary • Saffron • Sage • Thyme • Vanilla

1. Put all the flavoring ingredients into a pan and cover with around a quarter of the wine. For a sweet vermouth add the sugar at this stage.

2. Bring the liquid to a gentle simmer and keep it on low heat 10 minutes with the lid on, stirring occasionally.

3. Allow it to cool before adding the brandy. Pour the liquid and the botanicals into a clean, sterilized jar and leave overnight to infuse. It doesn't matter if the liquid doesn't fill the jar, as a slight oxidization adds to the authentic vermouth flavor.

4. Strain the mixture through a fine sieve or muslin cloth into a clean jar. To fully remove the bits of herbs and spices you'll have to strain it again through something finer, such as coffee filter paper.

5. Pour the remaining wine into the jar and taste. If the vermouth is a little too strong for your liking, you can add more wine until it suits your taste. If you think it could do with a flavor boost, pour a small quantity of vermouth into a pan and gently heat 10 minutes with the extra ingredients of your choice. Cool, strain and combine with the remaining vermouth. Similarly you may wish to add a teaspoon or two of sugar to a dry vermouth if you find it too bitter, or add more sugar to a sweet vermouth to match your preferences.

6. Keep notes of the flavorings you've used, and the next time you make it try some alternative ingredients from the list (see box).

Making time: 10 minutes | **Infusing time**: 2 to 24 hours

CHILI TEQUILA & MANGO MARGARITA

Nothing gets a party started like a shot of tequila—especially if you make it a twisted little firestarter with a blistering burst of chili. And where there's tequila, margaritas are sure to follow. We believe soft and seductive mango provides the perfect foil for our chili missiles— but it's your party, so add a dash of the hot stuff to whatever fruity number takes your fancy.

2 whole, fresh chilis
1 x 75cl bottle of tequila

FOR THE MARGARITA
2 tablespoons freshly prepared
   mango juice (see instructions)
2 tablespoon chili tequila
1 tablespoon triple sec
   or orange liqueur
1 teaspoon fresh lime juice
1 tablespoon salt
a pinch of chili flakes
a small wedge of lime

1. Choose your chilis wisely. Besides needing to make certain you can handle their heat, remember that they also possess subtly varying flavors. We like the sweet tomato heat that the Scotch Bonnet brings when we're playing with fire.

2. Make a few incisions in the chilis with the tip of a sharp knife, and drop them into a glass jar. Pour over the tequila.

3. The chilis should quickly begin to surrender their heat to the alcohol, so check the tequila after 2 hours. If your face contorts in pain, you should probably remove the chilis immediately; otherwise leave undisturbed for 24 hours before discarding them (and remember, it's easy to ratchet up the heat afterward by repeating the process with more chilis).

MANGO MARGARITA
4. Grab yourself a ripe, fresh mango. Peel it and slice the flesh from the stone. Dice to a purée in a blender and strain through a fine sieve to extract the juice.

5. Combine the thick mango juice with the tequila, triple sec, lime juice and some ice cubes in a cocktail shaker, or a jar with a well-fitting lid. Shake the jar at shoulder height like they do in the movies until the liquid is nice and cold.

6. Roughly mix the salt and chili flakes on a plate.

7. Rub the wedge of lime around the rim of your glass, then press it on to the salt and chili combo so it sticks to the rim.

8. Carefully pour the margarita into the glass. Take a deep breath. And drink.

RICH'S TIP
SET THE JUICE LOOSE
Put your limes in the microwave and cook for a few seconds on high to burst the juice-filled cells within. This will make them easier to squeeze and give you a higher juice yield.

Making time: 20 minutes | **Infusing time:** 1 month

ABSINTHE

Absinthe is not a drink to be messed with. Philosophers, artists and poets have all fallen foul of its infamous charms, with its psychotic and hallucinogenic properties being legendary.* Although the ingredients do include several psychedelic substances (see opposite), historical tales of crazed behavior were probably a result of the extremely high alcohol content in early distilled versions of the drink. Our recipe relies on infusion, and is centered around absinthe's "holy trinity" of anise, fennel and a variety of wormwood called *Artemisia absinthium*, from which the drink takes its name.

4 cardamom pods
2 teaspoons fennel seeds
2 teaspoons anise seeds
½ teaspoon coriander seeds
1½ teaspoons dried wormwood
1 star anise
½ teaspoon chamomile
1 teaspoon dried calamus root
2 large mint leaves
1 x 70cl bottle of vodka

1. Crack the cardamom pods and scrape out the seeds. Put these into the mortar with the fennel seeds, anise seeds and coriander seeds and crush them all with the pestle.

2. Scrape the crushed seeds into a jar or bottle. To this add the dried wormwood, star anise, chamomile and calamus root. The chamomile lends calming properties to the infusion (we rob a chamomile teabag of its contents); other recipes use lemon balm. If you can't find calamus root online or in your local pharmacy, it's no big deal if you leave it out.

3. Scrunch the mint leaves with your fingers so they begin releasing their oils, and drop these into your jar.

4. Cover the ingredients with the vodka and seal the jar. Give it a shake and leave it undisturbed in a cool, dark location around 1 month. Filter through a muslin cloth, and bottle.

SERVING SUGGESTIONS

Balance a special absinthe spoon (or teaspoon) across the rim of a small glass containing a shot (1 fluid ounce) of absinthe. Put a sugar cube on the teaspoon. Drizzle cold water over the sugar and wait until it's saturated. Resume water pouring so the sugar dissolves, spilling into the glass, until the drink is two-thirds water. Do not introduce fire—this is a modern gimmick designed to capitalize on absinthe's dubious reputation.

*In the late 19th century many artists, particularly those hanging out at Parisian cafés, believed absinthe could help stimulate their creativity. Henri de Toulouse-Lautrec relied on it so much that he kept a constant supply hidden within his walking cane, and when his drinking buddy, sunflower-dauber Vincent van Gogh, cut off part of his left ear absinthe was blamed—although many historians doubt this theory.

THE GREEN FAIRY

The most famous myth surrounding absinthe concerns visions of a green fairy, apparently caused by three potentially mind-altering substances. The most notorious, thujone, is present in wormwood; small amounts of antehole can be found in anise, fennel and star anise; and aserone is in calamus root—the ingredient said to give the fairy her green wings. Although traces of these substances are small in this recipe, please treat all ingredients with care.

🔩 HERBS & SPICES

The vast array of herbs and spices available to the modern cook can also be plundered by the home brewer and used for all types of drinks making. They can provide subtle flavor combinations in some drinks, or be the star of the show in others. They allow for endless creativity and experimentation.

GROWING AND SOURCING

Ever since humans began traveling, herbs and spices have been traded across the globe. These days there's a huge choice available, and most of the ingredients in this book will be easily accessible wherever you are in the world. Depending on your location, there are likely to be plenty you can pick fresh or even grow yourself. A pot of herbs on the windowsill is the simplest way to provide yourself with a ready source of fresh ingredients, while others can be easily grown outside in the yard. For some of the more unusual ingredients, such as wormwood, a quick scan of the Internet or trip to an pharmacy or herbalist might be in order.

USING HERBS AND SPICES

For many of the infusions and spiced drinks featured you'll need surprisingly small amounts of ingredients to impart the desired flavor. You'll also find that a few basic dried spices will keep for a long time, and can be used in many different drinks. Once you're comfortable using herbs and spices you can start to experiment. Instead of mint wine, try making wine using another leafy herb such as lemon balm. Or pep up simple recipes with classic cooking combinations—for example, raspberry and thyme is a pairing that has become fashionable among chefs, and we've used it for a whiskey infusion on page 120. Alternatively, you may wish to add a hit of ginger to a citrus infusion, a blast of basil to a honey recipe or drop a vanilla pod into your porter. Using herbs and spices opens up a whole new world of flavor.

PINCHES OF SPICE
OUR FAVORITE FIVE HERBS AND SPICES

Ginger: Most recipes will easily accommodate the spicy warmth of ginger. It can also be the main flavor in wine, beer and infusions. Buy fresh roots and store them in your refrigerator.

Cinnamon: The taste of Christmas. We prefer to use the dried sticks, but it's also available in powdered form.

Juniper berries: The main flavoring in gin, we use it to give a fresh, pine flavor to other drinks. If you're lucky you'll be able to pick the berries in the wild; otherwise, dried berries are readily available.

Mint: This is one of the easiest herbs to grow yourself. We've liberated mint from its familiar role as a cocktail garnish and built whole drinks around its fresh, clean flavor.

Wormwood: Often found in flower borders, the variety *Artemisia absinthium* gives absinthe both its flavor and its name. Available to buy dried for medicinal tea, it is also a key ingredient in vermouth and cocktail bitters.

Making time: 15 minutes | **Infusing time:** 3 days

HORSERADISH VODKA

As the popularity of endorphin-releasing foodstuffs such as chili and wasabi* increases, the humble horseradish seems to have been largely forgotten. But we're big fans of this riotous root, so when we read the words "horseradish vodka" in drinks-making maestro Andy Hamilton's excellent book *Booze for Free*, our eyes lit up. After running a few versions of his recipe we've settled on the combination of ingredients below. It's not the kind of tipple you gently sup to while away a few hours, but it's more than just a novelty drink. Besides giving sluggish sinuses a pick-me-up (just sniffing it gets the eyes watering) it can also be used to make a devilishly mean bloody Mary.

around 1 cup horseradish root, scrubbed or peeled and chopped into pinkie-finger-sized chunks
1 x 70cl bottle of vodka
1 teaspoon honey
15 whole black peppercorns

1. Drop the chopped horseradish into a jar with the vodka, honey and peppercorns. The honey will take away any slight bitterness of the root, and the peppercorns will add an extra layer of warmth. To help the honey dissolve more easily you can heat it with a fraction of the vodka or a touch of water before combining it with the other ingredients.

2. If you're desperate, you can strain and bottle this after 3 hours, but we recommend 3 days for maximum sinus-busting impact.

3. Keep in the freezer. Handle with care.

SERVING SUGGESTION
We like to drink our horseradish vodka Russian style: straight from the freezer, served neat, in a shot glass. Down in one and swiftly followed up with a pickled gherkin.

MAKER'S NOTES: GROW IT

Unlike its Japanese cousin, wasabi, horseradish is easy to grow. In fact it's so vigorous that its roots can quickly multiply and take over your whole veg plot. If you don't want to risk it running amok, confine it to a large pot. It's started by simply planting a piece of live root—readily available online or from most good garden centers—in winter or early spring, and can be harvested the following winter. Leave a few bits of root behind, and the process begins again.

*Wasabi is harder to grow than horseradish and more expensive to buy. Because of this, several sushi dips or snacks that are labeled "wasabi flavor" are actually a combination of horseradish and green coloring instead.

SPICED RUM

For nautical bounty hunters embarking on a long voyage of adventure, no grog fills a flagon better than spiced rum. But should a pirate wish to recreate his favorite spiced rum brand, of which there are many, he'll be met with the words "secret recipe" stamped on virtually every bottle. Fortunately for salty seadogs everywhere, we're happy to share our spiced rum secrets in this recipe, specially crafted to ward against the coldest lashings of wind and rain. If you think you can do better, then take your chances—vanilla and orange are the most frequently used flavors, but the rest of the spices are up for grabs, too.

1 x 70cl bottle of gold rum
1 vanilla pod
zest of ¼ orange
½ a cinnamon stick
1 star anise
4 black peppercorns
a pinch of ground nutmeg
4 coffee beans

ALTERNATIVE SPICES
allspice, cardamom, ginger,
 caraway, cloves, anise,
 rosemary, bay

1. First, choose your rum. We suggest an inexpensive golden rum—it'll have a bit more oak and caramel character than a silver or white rum, but won't be so aged that it overpowers the spices.

2. Split the vanilla pod and put it into a sterilized jar with the orange zest and the rest of the spices (including the coffee beans). If any of our suggested items don't appeal, swap them for something on the list of alternatives.

3. Pour the rum into the jar, seal it and give it a hard shake. Set aside around 2 weeks while you resume your hunt for buried treasure.

4. Filter the rum through a muslin cloth or fine sieve into bottles, hoist the colors and you're ready to splice the mainbrace in the spiciest of fashions.

SERVING SUGGESTIONS
This potent pirate potion can give an "arrrrr" to any number of drinks. Plunge a shot into a freshly brewed coffee, use it as a flavor boost in your favorite rum-based cocktail, add extra warmth to a hot toddy or try it instead of brandy in our classic egg-nog recipe on page 170.

Making time: 15 minutes | **Fermenting time**: 4 to 6 weeks | **Maturing time**: 1 month

MARROW RUM

This recipe is a great way to use up any unwanted marrows—the bloated, unloved relative of the zucchini and perennial surplus vegetable. While not strictly a "rum," of course, the taste of this deliciously dark veg-based booze will evoke thoughts of piratical high-seas adventure when the rich, velvety notes wash over your tongue and dance the hornpipe on your tonsils. What is also notable is the quirky fermentation method by which the drink is made. The sight of a trussed-up marrow, upturned and vulnerable in your kitchen, will certainly start (and stop) many conversations.

1 marrow—the largest you
  can find
2½ cups demerara sugar
1 tablespoon black treacle
1-inch piece gingerroot, peeled
  and grated
juice of 1 orange
red wine yeast

1. Take the marrow and slice off the top using a serrated knife, then scoop out the seedy innards with a spoon.

2. Stuff the marrow cavity with the sugar, treacle, ginger, orange juice and yeast. Standing the marrow upright in a pitcher will keep it steady.

3. Put the top back on the marrow and wrap it with parcel tape to keep it secure.

4. Keep the marrow upright in a pitcher or small fermenting bin and set aside somewhere warm. Your marrow may show signs of disintegration after 2 weeks. If so, wrap it in a muslin cloth tied with string, or put it in a (clean) pair of pantyhose.

5. After 4 weeks, your marrow should be ready to give up its juicy bounty. Pierce a hole in the bottom and allow the liquid to run into a fermentation jar.

6. Fit an airlock, then allow fermentation to finish before bottling (around 2 weeks).

7. This rummy treat will benefit from maturing, so try and leave it at least 1 month before sampling.

NAVAL GAZING
From 1655 until 1970, it was a British Royal Navy tradition for all enlisted men to receive a half-pint of rum a day. Alarmingly, this also included sailors serving aboard nuclear submarines!

ALTERNATIVELY . . .
Want some more nautical nonsense? Follow another navy tradition by making a scurvy-beating "marrow grog." Mix up 2 parts water to 1 part marrow rum, and add a dash of lime and a sprinkle of cinnamon for good measure.

Making time: 30 minutes | **Fermenting time:** 4 to 5 days | **Maturing time:** 1 to 2 weeks

ILZE'S BEET KVASS

It may not be the most alcoholic drink in our repertoire, but this veg-tastic Eastern European booze is perfect for using up surplus beets without reaching for the pickling jar. Kvass (derived from the Russian word meaning "sour") is treated as a medicinal tonic, believed to give the body a healthy pick-me-up, presumably to be imbibed before or after the commencement of any serious drinking. We've managed to wrestle this traditional beet recipe from our Latvian friend Ilze . . . it's one that has been passed down through the generations, and her family swear* by it. *"Prieka!"*

1⅛ pounds beets, washed, peeled
  and chopped into chunks
scant 1 cup sugar
juice and zest of 2 unwaxed
  lemons
ale yeast
1 rye bread slice, toasted
caraway seeds

1. Chuck the beet chunks into a fermenting bin. You can use grated beets if you like, as this will produce a faster ferment. However, we prefer to take it slow and steady.

2. Pour 16 cups boiling water over the beets (you may wish to use a kettle for this), then stir in the sugar, lemon zest and juice.

3. When cool, add the yeast and throw in a slice of toasted rye bread to add an authentic Soviet tang.

4. Mix everything together, cover with a lid or clean dish towel and leave to ferment quietly 4 to 5 days.

5. Strain the fermented liquid through a muslin cloth into sterilized bottles, dropping a few caraway seeds into each bottle for good measure.

6. Store the bottled kvass somewhere cool, then drink after 1 to 2 weeks' maturation. Marvel at its mild effervescence and magnificent magenta hue.

SOVIET THROWBACK

Although hugely popular in Communist-era Latvia, kvass disappeared from the streets after the breakup of the Soviet Union. New hygiene laws were introduced which prohibited sidewalk sales, and the market was quickly swamped and dominated by . . . Coca-Cola.

*In a good way, not a "What the @#&£& have you made this for?" way.

 **Making_time**: 30 minutes

EGG-NOG

It's the Christmas drink that divides opinion: some folks love it, some rank it alongside dry turkey and drunken aunts on their yuletide "avoid" list. Follow our easy steps to eggy heaven and discover that this oft-feared fusion of egg and booze should be celebrated, not scorned—for it is in fact a velvety-smooth creamy treat, and a most welcome festive guest.

2 large eggs, separated
scant ⅓ cup superfine sugar
½ a vanilla pod
2 cups whole milk
3 tablespoons vermouth
3 tablespoons brandy
grated nutmeg, to taste

1. Squeeze a chicken until it dispenses 2 eggs. Alternatively, ask a friendly farmer, or purchase a box from your local grocery store and extract two.

2. Whisk the egg yolks and sugar together in a bowl until creamy and smooth.

3. Scrape the seeds from the vanilla pod into the milk. You can also add the seeded pod, but remember to remove it before serving.

4. Heat the milk gently in a saucepan, removing it from the heat just before it boils. Carefully pour the hot milk into the egg and sugar mixture, whisking to combine.

5. Pour the mixture back into the saucepan, then continue to whisk over gentle heat until it starts to thicken.

6. Add the vermouth and brandy, give it a whisk, then remove from the heat.

7. Beat the egg whites in a bowl until stiff peaks form. (Unless you possess gorilla-like forearms, use an electric whisk.) Pour in the egg and milk mixture, and combine.

8. Spoon into cups, then chill before serving with a festive flourish of nutmeg.

MAKER'S NOTES:
USE YOUR NOG

Egg-nog also crops up in a number of fashionable boozes—see our rhubarb and custard cocktail on page 129 as an example. But don't store your "nog" in the cupboard with the rest of your cocktail potions—for safety's sake, refrigerate and drink within 2 days.

Making time: 20 minutes | **Infusing time**: 45 minutes

GLÖGG

Adding spices to wine before serving it hot is a popular pursuit the world over. The most globally familiar term for this form of booze is "mulled wine", but many countries and regions have their own named versions, which include smoking bishop (England), glühwein (Germany and Austria) and caribou (Canada). However, our favorite is the Swedish variant glögg (also known as gløgg in Norway), a potent mix of red wine, port and wintry spices served with slivered almonds and raisins. So, why not treat any shivering friends to our recipe for this warming tipple, and summon a hearty "*skål**" to the good folk of Sweden.

1 x 75cl bottle of red wine
½ a bottle (1½ cups) port
6 cardamom pods, cracked
2-inch piece gingerroot, peeled
   and roughly chopped
12 cloves
1 cinnamon stick
zest of ½ an orange
½ cup brandy or rum

TO SERVE
raisins
slivered almonds
orange peel
sugar, to taste

1. Pour the wine and port into a pan. Scrape the cardamom seeds into the liquid, discarding the empty husks.

2. Add the ginger to the pan along with the cloves, cinnamon stick and orange zest (avoid the pith).

3. Heat the liquid until it's just shy of boiling point. Remove the pan from the heat, cover with a lid and set aside to infuse 45 minutes.

4. Strain the liquid and return it to the pan. Increase the already heady alcohol content to even boozier heights by adding the brandy or rum.

5. When you're ready to serve the glögg, gently warm the liquid before pouring it into your grateful recipients' mugs.

6. Sprinkle a few raisins, slivered almonds and thin strips of orange peel into each cup, and provide a bowl of sugar in case any imbibers wish to sweeten their hot, intoxicating brew.

"Cheers!"

INDEX

Acknowledgments

Thanks for...
Tasting, critiquing and words of encouragement: Kerry, Catherine, Daisy, Emily, Jo, Julia, Jim, David, Janet, Geoff, Linda, Adam, Lisa, Gary, Jade, Dav, Cath, Graham, Ollie, Simon, Alison, Cat, Larry, Steve, Damian.
Advice, inspiration or sheer enthusiasm for our madness: Diana Jackson, Ben Hardy, Gary & Pete, Neil Worley, Andy Hamilton, Sarah Comber, Chelsea Monroe-Cassel, Andy Jones,

Trevor Witt, Kester Bunyon, Carl Legge, Simon Gladding.
Getting the book together: Jane, Grace, Rebecca, Georgie, Liz.
Thanks also to Marion and Paul at Barrington Pottery, Christine Brain at Barrington Court, Camilla and Amanda at Vigo, Darren and Andrew at the London Distillery, Peter Pomphrey, Seamus Coyle, Martin Hopkins and the Watsons for their apples, Gerard, Juliet and Bob at Honey's Cider.

And finally an apology to anyone who suffered from trying our first attempt at absinthe (too much wormwood), the dodgy batch of cider (unidentified rogue apple), the trial pea pod wine (rejected) and anyone within five miles of the revolting banana beer. It won't happen again.

Nick & Rich
www.twothirstygardeners.co.uk

CAMERON + COMPANY

Cameron + Company is a boutique publishing house, creating and distributing "books that need to be books" since 1964 with a focus on photography, art, food + wine, children's and publications of regional interest. Visit us at **www.cameronbooks.com.**